FAILURE
WITHOUT
FEAR

An educator's guide
to supporting all students

Chad Reay

FAILURE WITHOUT FEAR

An educator's guide to supporting all students

Edited by Darrin Griffiths, EdD
Copyedited by Ruth Bradley
Book design by Jim Bisakowski – www.bookdesign.ca

ISBN 978-0-9959782-5-6

Word & Deed Publishing Incorporated
1860 Appleby Line, Suite #778
Burlington, Ontario, Canada, L7L 7H7
(Toll Free) 1-866-601-1213

Visit our website at
www.wordanddeedpublishing.com

Acknowledgements

I would first like to thank my amazing wife Emma. She has shaped the way I think about education and is the first one to support a new idea and encourage me to "give it a go." Her amazing ability to listen and sift through my jumbled thoughts is a true gift. Without her passionate involvement, input, and support this book would not have been possible.

I must express my very profound gratitude to my parents and to my brothers and sister for providing me with unfailing support and continuous encouragement. They have always modelled exceptional family values that I will carry forward. My parents never had an "agenda" for me, but always honoured me for who I am.

I would also like to thank Cheryl Van Ooteghem, Superintendent of Education, for her dedication and support. She always pushes my thinking and challenges my status quo. She was always available when I had a quick question or idea and was willing to sit through in-depth discussions about topics that others may not have wanted to debate. Cheryl's keen interest and outside-the-box thinking have encouraged me always to fail on.

Finally, many thanks to my two amazing boys. They regularly say, "I've found a key and unlocked another mystery about myself," which has encouraged me to continue to unlock mysteries about myself every day — and to find the persistence to press on while writing this book. Their built-in curiosity and natural inquisitiveness encourage me to help shape the best education system I can for them to prosper in whatever they choose to do.

Thank you all. I hope you enjoy reading and working through the book as much as I enjoyed writing it.

Contents

Foreword

By Jenni Donohoo

There are lessons to be learned from all kinds of failure. When failures are considered epic and consequences far reaching, lessons tend to cross cultures and permanently change the way people think and behave. Lessons learned from moderate failure can be equally impactful for individuals. The key concept here is that learning from failure occurs because lessons are identified through recognition, analysis, and reflection.

In this book, Chad Reay explores what it means to fail and how to learn from our mistakes. Failure is often equated with quitting, or signifies the end of a dream. Here, readers are encouraged to take a different perspective, and embrace failure as a positive rather than a negative, by considering how failure is a necessary process to achieving ultimate success.

Too often in schools, mistakes are used to measure students' academic achievement. In other words, when students make a mistake, their grades are negatively impacted. Reay encourages readers to examine a different purpose for errors and rather than use mistakes to measure worth, use them as a vehicle for developing deeper understanding. Educators will make many personal connections to the experiences and stories about how failure can help lead people to success. In addition, there are many practical ideas offered for what educators can do to embrace failure themselves and to help their students understand the value in errors.

Educators can create the conditions for their students — and for each other — to be comfortable with and responsible for surfacing learning from failure. They can create a culture where lessons are learned through recognition, analysis, and reflection in search of a deep under-standing of what happened when things go wrong. This is Chad Reay's vision for schools and classrooms. While this vision is a reality in many cases, there are still opportunities for teachers and students to re-con-ceptualize failure. Reay begins to paint that picture in this resource.

Jenni Donohoo is a Provincial Literacy Lead, on contract with the Council of Ontario Directors of Education. In this role, she works with system and school leaders in order to support high-quality professional learning and improve adolescent literacy.

Introduction

So why this book, at this time? Why would I sit down and write about failure, such a negative and difficult topic, and one that generally makes people anxious as soon as they hear the word? As an experienced educator, I have travelled across our district and come to the same conclusion year after year — we don't allow our children enough opportunities to fail! It's as if we want to treat our education system like the local Ford plant, a production line of children who can spit out perfect answers and robotic responses. This is designed to appease us and reaffirm educators that indeed, we are doing a marvelous job, but is it properly preparing students for their futures? Often as educators, we jump to rescue students by answering questions for them without giving them time to think, perhaps make a mistake, reflect, and then truly learn from that experience. Situations can become even more complex when parents get involved, fearful, or upset about a child's "failure." I started asking myself how we are helping *all* children be successful if they aren't allowed to fail gracefully, especially when education systems continue to treat failure as the true "F" word. It felt like a missing resource for us, as educators, was something that addressed this fear of failure.

For me, my first memory of failure was getting cut from my local hockey team when I was 10. Obviously, there were failures prior to that in life, but that one still stands out to this day. Something about the complete and utter disappointment of knowing that I was not going to be able to play with my best friends, or be a part of the cool crowd, just stuck with me. How would people look at me now that I was such a failure? Would I be allowed to go to their birthday parties? Would people think I was a loser? I even thought that my family would be so disappointed in me that I would have to live somewhere else. I mean, the world literally felt like it was coming to a halt right in front of my eyes. What was I going to do?

In addition, at this time I was in French Immersion while all my other friends were in the English stream. My failure to make the hockey team became another layer on what felt like a weighted blanket on my shoulders. To make it worse, I was also finding difficulties in areas that my friends were having no trouble with — simple things like reading! To hear other kids my age reading beautifully, in my mind, was a constant reminder that I was a failure in comparison.

Siblings too played a factor. Having siblings that were both older and younger meant that I was always trying to impress one of them with either what I could do or what I knew. Siblings, being siblings, don't often acknowledge your self-professed awesomeness. As you grow and start to establish who you are, it is therefore not uncommon to experience failure — especially regarding older siblings. And of course, teenage failure can feel rather harsh and dramatic!

What I learned from these experiences, however, has had a profound effect on me as an adult. Collectively, what these failures allowed me to do was to meet new friends, travel to new places, learn how other people work together as part of a team, motivate myself to work harder, and realize that those "life and death" failures were really just temporary setbacks. In fact, they made me more resilient, better at managing my emotions, and overall a more mindful human.

The thought process behind writing this book began when I was working at a Young Offenders facility in a custody unit. During my ten years there, I worked in various roles; however, the role that pushed me into education was as a social worker, working in section 23 (then section 19) classrooms. These are educational facilities for students who have been suspended for lengthy periods, or even expelled. I saw demoralization in the eyes of every student there, based on repetitive failures. These children believed they were failures to their families, parents, schools, society, and themselves. This constant strain started wearing on me too. I truly believed that our team could start making a difference in the education of these young people — after all, they were under our care for six months — if we created an environment where mistakes were accepted and adversity was simply part of the learning journey. In some cases, school itself was a trigger for explosive behavioural outbursts, and that was my starting point for trying to address failure as a *positive*, rather than a negative. The classroom teacher and I started to collaborate about ways to talk about, plan for, expect, and accept failure as a necessary part of learning. Although we had our successes, we also had failures of our own.

Ironically, one of our failures resulted from our failure to mention to a new student admitted to the program that we embraced failure as part of learning. That morning we came prepared to class expecting an amazing morning of learning and assessment. We had deliberately planned an open-ended lesson that would create cognitive dissonance and encourage teamwork. As the lesson began, I noticed that our new student wasn't coping well and was getting quite vocal in his frustration. Just then, I heard our model student (charged with grand-theft auto, joyriding, and assaulting a police officer) say, "I love this and I don't mind failing." I knew this wasn't going to be received well by our new resident, but I didn't expect what happened next. This new student, who had just finished animatedly using his diverse vocabulary to express his frustration, seemingly calmly responded by saying, "I don't, I get worksheets and work quietly!" Then he picked up a desk, swung it around like a hammer-throwing athlete, and released it in the direction of the chalkboard. I had no idea that a slate blackboard would shatter like a pane of glass and sound like two cars hitting head-on at full speed. To this day, that was one of the most thought-provoking things I have ever witnessed in a classroom (nobody was hurt), and I suspect one of the most adverse responses to failure in education ever! That situation has provided me with a constant reminder that we need to ask students about how we can best help them be successful, not assume that as adults and educators we automatically know. Years later, this realization was still affecting me tremendously in my career.

During my time as a social worker, I spent much effort liaising with elementary and secondary schools in transition planning for students to go back into their local community school. These were difficult meetings, as the local schools were always hesitant to accept our students back into the regular stream for fear of what could happen. When we would share the student's success or embarrassing failures at school and how we worked through it as a process, I would often be met with, "We don't have time for failure with the curriculum as big as it is." Or, "That's nice in a class of 8, but not in a class of 30." One school representative said, "She's already a failure to our system, so can't you house her for the next few years? That way it won't affect our scores." Although I was tremendously frustrated, I was taught at a very young age to turn frustration into motivation and use it as the fuel to make change. (Thanks Mom and Dad!) This incident became one of my motivating factors in trying to change our approach to education.

Despite that backdrop of teaching that failure isn't to be feared, once I became a classroom teacher, I was as guilty as anyone of not allowing my students sufficient opportunity to productively fail their way through their learning. I was constantly worried about getting "through" and "covering" the curriculum, and I wasn't patient enough to use rich tasks and feedback to allow students to fail their way towards understanding their learning styles. I also got caught up in the notion of underestimating the ability of my students, who primarily came from low socioeconomic areas of the inner city.

After eight years in the classroom, I accepted a job with the Ontario Ministry of Education. In my role as a Student Work Study Teacher, I did grassroots action research with struggling students. I spent intensive amounts of time in Kindergarten to Grade 8 classrooms shadowing and interviewing students to research what their roadblocks were as they learned. This was all done through the lens of the student, not the teacher. Once I collected this information, I would work with the classroom teachers to develop specific lessons to address those needs and close the gaps. For example, one student was struggling to identify what a mathematical word problem was asking them to do. My job was to probe deeper into this area. This allowed me to spend time asking if it was specific vocabulary, operational, or a matter of not knowing where to start. These specific questions allowed the classroom teacher and me to plan targeted mini-lessons or guided small group sessions to begin to address these areas of concern. This was an amazing role, learning how to take a step back, listen and learn from the students, and truly hear the "student voice." This specific one-year role changed the way I viewed our education system and the way we deliver curriculum.

In my role as a Curriculum Leader, held over a period of five years, I had the great fortune of supporting all 64 elementary schools in our district — both rural and urban. My experiences ranged from supporting French Immersion schools, Kindergarten to Grade 3, 6, and 8 schools, and supporting "section" schools that work with students who have been removed from their home schools for behavioural reasons. I primarily led and supported our school board in the areas of mathematics and language; however, over the course of my five years I also led the Equity and Inclusion, ESL, Science and Technology, and Student Success (Kindergarten to Grade 6) portfolios. This wide variety of experiences opened my eyes to how administrators, teachers, and students respond to risk taking and the notion of change. It became apparent very quickly that I needed to model failure. What did that look like in a teacher-leader role? It was not part of our educational fabric to try something and have it not go well. There was obvious discomfort from teachers when lessons didn't go exactly as planned, when children acted out because a new person was in the class, when children were speaking when they should be listening, when technology failed to co-operate, or when students didn't understand what was being taught the first time. The concept of designing innovative lessons where students were challenged to problem solve, communicate, fail, revise, try again, and maybe still not produce the perfectly desired outcome — according to *our* education standards — was intriguing to me. The moment I overheard, "This is making me feel uncomfortable. Can't we just give them the answer and stop the struggle? It's painful to sit back and watch!" I knew I had to pursue the idea of positive failure — and maybe even write a book to move us towards a more student-focused approach to education. After all, as educators we care about our students. We want them to do well in school and learn as much as they can. We want them to love learning, and to be resourceful and persistent in the face of challenges. We don't want our students to lose heart when they get stuck, make mistakes, or receive disappointing grades.

Currently I am vice-principal in a Kindergarten–Grade 8 French Immersion school of approximately 630 students and 50 staff members. I truly believe that apart from the importance of relationship building, demonstrating on a daily basis how to work through, around, and past failure is crucial for our school to be successful. Acknowledging that we will all fail as teachers, principals and vice-principals, students, office coordinators, caretakers, parents, and human beings has facilitated our safe and healthy environment to try new things, to take risks with the full understanding that it may not go well. This approach, especially when layered with the expectation to "Be the Best You," means that when we try new initiatives or strategies and fail, we take advantage of learning from our mistakes. In my experience, this allows us to get better at refining our efforts to be the best that we can all be — no matter what our roles are. I believe that this is a critical time to re-evaluate and shift the paradigm from rote, results-based learning to a bigger-picture approach — one where teaching students how to learn through the failures of fearlessly trying new things creates more dynamic and confident members of society.

Another reason I believe in the importance of failure without fear is that the consequences of education systems that don't create safe and inclusive environments in which to make mistakes and learn from them go beyond how well students learn. Education is a strong predictor of health (Freudenberg & Ruglis, 2007). Creating a better environment for our students will directly impact dropout rates. Completing high school opens the gateway to higher education and thus to better-paid jobs. Higher education also contributes to better-informed health choices, and is associated with higher levels of social support (Freudenberg & Ruglis, 2007). Consequently, dropping out of school may reduce access to several health-promoting resources and increase the risk of negative health behaviours such as the use of tobacco, alcohol, illicit drugs, and attempted suicide (Bachman et al., 2008; Maynard, Sala-Wright, & Vaughn, 2015; Swain, Beauvais, Chavez, & Oetting, 1997; Townsend, Flisher, & King, 2007; Wichstrøm, 1998). Viewed through this lens, we understand the absolute urgency to learn more about failure so that we can help students become successful.

The intention behind this book is to provide anyone who works in education with a different way of thinking about how we can better support student learning by changing our approach to teaching. Although it includes specific examples to help support student learning, this book is not meant to be a teachers' manual. The idea is to provide you, the educator, with a different perspective on a concept that is not often addressed with adults or kids. This wealth of strategies for educators to try at the system, school, and classroom level, however, are dependent on your level of comfort and flexibility within your current situation. Since education systems are supposed to revolve around doing what's best for kids, it's inevitable that I provide you with strategies to help you change your education landscape.

Throughout this book, I explore ways to help you avoid falling into the same trap that I did, one that leads to questions from your students like, "Why don't I have time to do this again to get better?" Truthfully, when he asked that question I thought, "Damn, he's right!" My only response at the time was, "I think it's best we just move on, otherwise we will be stuck on this concept forever!" This was probably the worst response I could have given him, although it does illustrate that I too am failing my way through my career in order to do better next time.

I encourage you to read this book with the goal of becoming comfortable taking your own risks. You may choose to read it individually, although I strongly suggest that you make it the focus of group study. A collaborative and consistent message from classroom to classroom can only benefit students. The questions for guidance and reflection that conclude each chapter make it ideal for book studies, book clubs, virtual sharing spaces, or any other collaborative form of reading.

My challenge to you: Seriously consider how you can change some of your existing philosophies to embrace the idea of "Failure Without Fear" — and give your students the time, space, and support to do the same.

Chapter 1

What is Failure?

We must own, trust and respect failure before we can get the most out of it.

—Anjali Sastry and Kara Penn, *Fail Better*

noun fail·ure \āfāl-yər\ (Webster's)

1a: omission of occurrence or performance; *specifically* **: a failing to perform a duty or expected action** <*failure* **to pay the rent on time>**
1b (1): a state of inability to perform a normal function <**kidney** *failure*> **— compare heart failure**
1b (2): an abrupt cessation of normal functioning <a power *failure*>
1c: a fracturing or giving way under stress <structural *failure*>

2a: lack of success : a failing in business : bankruptcy

3a: a falling short : deficiency <a crop *failure*>
3b: deterioration, decay

4: one that has failed

Have you ever wondered what society would look like, and specifically what our education system would look like, sound like, or feel like, if we looked at failure as an opportunity to grow? What if teachers and schools spent more time with students developing better self-confidence, resiliency, and the ability to take risks, instilling in them the idea that failure is an acceptable part of the learning process? What if we valued mistakes and flipped our perception of failure on its head? Rather than frowning upon failure and shaming it, what if we encouraged children to consistently identify what went wrong in order to grow and build upon learning as part of a reflective inquiry cycle? This approach would reduce the anxiety of being wrong and encourage positive mental health amongst staff and students. If educators were to establish positive relationships with students, allowing them to take risks without being judged or criticized for not being perfect, then we would better prepare students to be more innovative and creative. Educators who provide emotional support at school and who create a safe and inclusive environment better allow students to flourish in their own individual ways. Once students start to receive ongoing feedback from teachers about ways to move past or around barriers, they begin to become more resilient. When students realize that it's okay to make mistakes — to fail — they can persevere through tasks and start to unlock their potential one experience at a time.

I'm not saying this is easily accomplished, as evidenced by looking at some common fears amongst educators. I'm often told that if we use the word "failure" with children then they will start to believe that they are one; that if we talk about it being okay to fail in the classroom then students will be less likely to perform to the best of their abilities. After all, educational institutes are meant to promote success, so how can we risk stunting potential by teaching students how to fail? On top of that, if we use failure in dialogue with parents then they might think we are being negative towards their children, and we run the risk of them disengaging with us as professionals. I believe that these common assumptions — these perceived barriers — are the exact reasons why we need to actively change our thought processes about these two powerful words: fail and failure.

At the beginning of this chapter, I gave a dictionary definition of the word "failure." However, given that throughout this book the words fail and failure will appear frequently, it's important to understand what *I* mean by them. A starting point is to spend some time unpacking what I *do not* mean by failure in education. When I refer to failure, or to Failure Without Fear, it does not refer to the following concepts:

- Failing a grade or failing to earn credits
- Failing at being profitable in business
- Categorizing or marginalizing certain demographics or profiles of students (poverty, race, religion, students with exceptionalities, gender)
- Failing to graduate on time
- A failed marriage or relationship-based failures
- Failing a test

So then what *do* I mean when I speak about fear and failure? Failure Without Fear describes a system of values; a mindset and approach that is meant to be liberating for both educators and students. Failure — viewed through this lens — opens doors and begins conversations, allowing children and adults the opportunity to think critically and innovatively. Failure, to me, is a temporary setback in the learning process, one that acts as a short-term hurdle on your way to completing a task or achieving a goal.

The Many Sides of Failure

Identifying the root of a student's failure can help them either to overcome a similar challenge or obstacle in the future, or help us, as educators, better know how to work with them and turn past failures into successes. This can be challenging given that failure has many roots and forms. Failure can be content-based, process-based, or relationship-based. It can be singular, or a combination of these. It can be caused or influenced both internally and externally.

Here are some examples of what failure could look like:

- Is it process-based, such as a student who completely understood the content of a unit but failed to communicate their learning on paper?
- Is it content-based, such as when a student just can't grasp the ideas no matter how the content is being presented?
- Is it relationship-based, such as when a student performs amazingly well in one class but is unable to perform at peak levels in another class despite there being no issues with understanding the content? Is this the student's problem or is it a teacher problem?
- Is it an internal issue, such as when a student has failed previously at something and is lacking the confidence to try again?
- Is it influenced by external factors out of the student's control, such as selection committees, teachers assessing arbitrarily, or coaches who select teams based on prior relationships — or even nepotism?

Identifying the root cause or type of failure will help students mentally prepare to accept and learn from those failures. The first step in being able to support students as they fail forward is to change our own approach as educators. If we don't understand how people process learning, we often assume that the final product is all they are capable of. This can mean that we sometimes miss the most important part of the learning process — the messiness of asking questions, trying out new concepts, getting it wrong, learning from those setbacks, and reapplying that knowledge to new situations. It is crucial that we get to know our students in order to decipher their content, process, or relationship struggles to best support them. If we don't understand how students process failure, we are often unable to help them through their situation.

We know that students fail for various reasons. Even when they think they are good at something, failure may occur due to circumstances beyond their control. It's what happens next that we need to focus on. For example, if a selection committee does not accept a student into a program, that student is forced to make choices about their education based on external forces. This may mean taking another avenue towards their goal, asking for feedback to make improvements to reapply and find success, or, depending on their level of resiliency and exposure to adversity, stopping. As educators — and simply as adults who have lived through more experiences — we know that failure can make us stronger and more determined to reach our goals, even if it means a change in plans. That persistence and determination, I believe, is greater in people who have failed along the way than in those who found the "game of school" too easy. Essentially, some students are never pushed to their full potential. Without tasks and activities that require critical thinking, they simply conform to norms, routines, and expectations, and therefore don't fail often enough. It is incumbent on us to create environments where failure is accepted, and perhaps even sought after, depending on the circumstances.

Peter Senge, named one of the "World's Top Management Gurus" by the *Financial Times* in 2000, does a nice job of defining failure as "a shortfall, evidence of the gap between vision and current reality. Failure is an opportunity for learning about inaccurate pictures of current reality, about strategies that didn't work as expected, about the clarity of a vision of a goal" (Senge, 2006, p. 143). This definition implies that failure is in the eye of the beholder, and can vary from person to person, depending on their mindset and the surrounding environment. It follows then that the impact of a school or classroom environment is critical in defining failure. Garfield Gini-Newman suggests that if educators take a "fail forward," inquiry-based approach in which failure is embraced as an opportunity for further learning and not as a shortcoming, our classrooms become much more rich and dynamic (Gini-Newman, 2014). He goes on to say that students often fail to see the connections between their daily lessons and the intended broad learning outcomes, leading to questions of relevance and a perception that ongoing formative assessment has little value.

Often students devote most of their efforts towards achieving marks or grades. When the ask if what they are doing is for marks they really want to know if it's worth their investment of time to complete the task. We often link this to students being unmotivated but really we need to be mindful that students need to understand the link between their daily lessons, the feedback they receive and that everything they do contributes to a deeper understanding of the task they are doing rather than it just being for marks (Gini-Newman, 2014, pg. 4) More importantly, we need to use this opportunity to reinforce the idea that getting good grades isn't the only indicator of success, and that failure on the way to truly understanding something is not only acceptable but also more desirable than getting it right the first time but not knowing how to do it again.

It's also interesting to think about how our pathways and outcomes in life are influenced, especially in light of this critical shift in outlook. We assume that our successes are the most important aspect of our experiences, yet I would argue that our failures, more often than not, allow us to make decisions about our learning and our goals. For example, although some people may have pursued their dream job or career following a perfect pathway through elementary, secondary, and postsecondary school, my belief is that these people are rare. Most of us feel our way along through trial and error, learning from our mistakes, our failures, and our bad luck to better determine what to eliminate as options from our career path. From a very young age, children start to weigh their options, figuring out what they are good at and not so good at. In most cases, people fail their way towards their passion. Experiencing certain workplace realities helps us eliminate paths along the way as we realize that those types of environments might not be for us. Perhaps the terrible heat in a restaurant kitchen, sitting behind a desk for too long, or a job so boring that you feel like your brain is petrifying have dissuaded you from certain careers. Or perhaps you know exactly what you want to do but keep failing, and then get up again and keep trying. In a 1995 interview, Steve Jobs alluded to his many failures, saying, "I'm convinced that about half of what separates the successful entrepreneurs from the non-successful ones is pure perseverance." Therefore, fail on my friends!

All too often we educators are so driven by outdated unit quizzes, exams, and standardized test scores that we have trouble allowing the time required for children to be reflective, to revisit their failures — and actually learn from them. Report card marks, test scores, and final exams seem to be the definitive way in which the "system" deems success or failure, along with such things as graduation rates, college or university acceptance, and apprenticeship entry. In Ontario, for example, standardized tests in Grades 3, 6, and 9 are mandated by the Education Quality and Accountability Office (EQAO) responsible for the provincial assessment program. As stated on their website[1], "EQAO assesses how well Ontario's public education system is developing students' reading, writing and math skills. EQAO provides reliable and useful information that is used to help improve student achievement and ensure the accountability of school boards."[1] The challenge can be that because the results don't "count for marks," students might not really be giving their best effort. Alternately, they might really care about doing well and put additional stress on themselves. In neither case, however, do they truly learn what success or failure means based on the outcome of their result?

Since most people fail their way towards their passion, a system focused only on results, with no room to talk about or learn from failure, is at odds with how success actually works. Day to day — from entering Kindergarten to exiting Grade 12 — we fixate on not making mistakes, despite the fact that students' post-schooling experiences are what determines their path. In a society that uses job rates and unemployment statistics as measures of success and failure, then, despite the awareness that students have years to prepare for their life outside of school, we need to ask if our current approach is working. So, do we need to stop attaching grades to student work? We will examine this later in the book, but the idea of embracing failure is paramount. I suggest that we deal with failure on a moment-by-moment basis, looking at these stumbles in learning as productive opportunities for students to build on what they failed at and apply their new learning to similar future problems. If we deal with success and failure in this manner, the test-score-driven success markers take care of themselves; moreover, we would not only see improvements in these results, we would see improvements in student wellbeing and mental health.

---

1   http://www.eqao.com/

Education systems must do a better job of incorporating failure as part of assessment practices and also of sharing assessment information with children through a different lens; one through which we give students opportunities to learn and grow, all while linking the process to everyday life. This may mean zooming out to look holistically at how assessment practices are implemented and executed. As teachers, we determine student success or failure by arbitrarily assigning grades; in so doing, we often push the students who don't fit our system out the door, effectively setting them up for failure outside of school as well. In the true concept of learning, however, nobody fails. Economic realities may make it difficult to envision a different paradigm, but imagine shifting our thinking in the ways these questions suggest:

- What if students started a movement demanding the opportunity to struggle without being deemed a failure?
- What if students all identified themselves as strong, capable learners wishing to be taught based specifically on their individual needs, not compared to each other?
- What if students started to challenge us all to deliver modern, content-rich programs leveraged with technology support?
- How could pre-service teaching institutions better prepare educators for this approach?

I believe that each student should have an individual education plan (IEP), crafted in part by their own input. Under such a system, differentiation would no longer be done through streaming of courses. Can we imagine such a system, where students are assertive and empowered enough to ensure that that their goals are being met by educators instead of the other way around? In such a system, educators would pay attention to the social wellbeing of students, to their need to feel safe enough in the learning environment to explore different ways and discover what approaches suit them best in different circumstances.

As a father, is it socially acceptable for me to allow my children to shut down and avoid failure? Do I constantly shelter them from it, or do I support their opportunities to experience the curveballs of day-to-day life, develop the ability to pick themselves up, recover from the setback, and try again? I believe it is my moral obligation to teach them how to respect failure, not fear it. If this is true of us as parents, then it should be true of us as educators — it's just a matter of how.

Determining to support students as they learn to fail without fear is only one step though. How can we better equip ourselves to capture opportunities where students have not been successful in their first, second, or even third attempt? How can we help students identify their own misconceptions about their shortcomings and about what they can do well? How do we push students to grow and flourish, and to celebrate the fact that they took a risk, asked more questions, and had the fortitude to persevere? How do we support students and teach them to accept failure as a step toward success, particularly in a healthy risk-taking manner? I challenge us all to start thinking about this now. As you continue reading, remember that failure is no longer a negative word; instead, it fuels motivation, creativity, and future success. As Wayne Gretzky once said, "The day I stop learning is the day I stop growing. You miss 100% of the shots you don't take."

In the chapters that follow, we will examine how shifts in attitudes, beliefs, and mindsets can help students and adults learn from failure and propel their learning forward. We will look into data to help us make informed decisions and guide education systems more towards a child-centred approach. We will also focus on the importance of technological integration and how new teachers can benefit from the idea that failure allows us to learn and grow as part of a process; it is not a state of being.

Ideas to try with colleagues or in the classroom

Discuss your thoughts about how failure can be content-, process-, or relationship-based, or can be influenced by external forces, and how this will better help you understand your students

Ask yourself and your colleagues from different cultures and backgrounds, "What does failure mean to you?" Keep track of the data and use a Wordle to display it. This will help to build your own social context about what students are experiencing.

Take the opportunity to ask students, "What does failure mean to you?" at the beginning of the year. Record their answers and then have them discuss and reflect on them at the end of the year. Have their answers changed over the year as you work towards productive failures?

Chapter 2

Understanding Different Mindsets

Expect chaos, and plan accordingly. Anticipate what will go wrong and plan for how you will address it.

—Chris Hadfield

This chapter will guide us through the ideas behind growth, fixed, and flexible mindsets, and how mindset affects how a person responds to adverse situations, either promoting or hindering their own learning. The first step is to understand what each state of mind means. Before we can properly connect a person's mindset with their approach to failure, we must understand the differences in how people think. It is important to reflect on how we navigate the world around us and how we approach new learning opportunities to best equip ourselves for optimal outcomes. If acceptance — and even promotion — of failure is desirable, then which way of thinking — which mindset — is most desirable? This chapter will help put us in the right mindset to take risks, make mistakes, and feel comfortable with failure as an opportunity to promote personal growth. By doing so, we increase our chances of dealing with adversity in a constructive rather than destructive manner.

Growth versus Fixed Mindset

A growth mindset is the belief that you can develop your talents and abilities through hard work, good strategies, and help from others. It stands in opposition to a fixed mindset, which is the belief that talents and abilities are unalterable traits, ones that can never be improved. Recent studies by members of the Mindset Scholars Network found that students who have been taught to believe that intelligence can grow over time (a growth mindset) perform better in school than students who have been taught to believe that intelligence is a fixed trait determined at birth (a fixed mindset; see Romero, 2015).

The links between mindsets and achievement received important new validation from studies by mindset scholars Carol Dweck and Dave Paunesku, and Stanford education researcher Susana Clar (Bowermaster, 2016, para. 4). The concept of a growth mindset was originally conceived by Professor Carol Dweck of Stanford University. Dweck states that an individual's learning is shaped by whether they believe their intelligence is fixed and static, or whether they believe their intelligence can grow, change, and alter. In a fixed mindset, learners believe that their basic qualities, such as intelligence or talent, are fixed traits. They spend their time documenting their intelligence or talent instead of developing it. They also believe that talent alone creates success — without effort. Students with a fixed mindset believe that their basic abilities are static and that each person was born with a certain amount of ability; therefore, effort put into achieving goals is worthless (Dweck, 2006; 2012).

Professor Hattie, Director of the Melbourne Education Research Institute, says the most appropriate situations for using a growth mindset are "when we do not know an answer, when we make an error, when we experience failure [and] when we are anxious" (Hazell, 2017, para. 8). When we don't know an answer — or even where to begin — it's crucial to be flexible in our thinking and allow ourselves permission to try new strategies. This can signal to us that the problem can be solved with effort and intention. He argues, however, that there are other situations where it is inappropriate and can even impede learning: "Having a growth mindset... may not be needed for easy tasks, or on performance of tasks that are 'novel and ill-defined and that therefore require both creativity and the willingness to abandon unsuccessful strategies'" (Hazell, 2017, para. 10).

The helpfulness of a growth mindset was made clear to me when I worked with a student diagnosed with a memory retention deficit. Rather than using it as an excuse, she began to think of ways to make learning more accessible in her own unique way. She demonstrated her growth mindset by using technology to screenshot specific procedures (logging on to her computer, accessing her math folder, attaching files to her emails) that she needed to use on a daily basis so she could access them easily from any device rather than continuously forget the procedure and be unable to complete her work. This growth mindset allowed her to become more productive.

However, "there is no general state to aim for called 'I have a growth mindset,'" says Hattie, "as we can have both fixed and growth, they have advantages at different times" (Hazell, 2017, para. 12). An example of a student struggling due to her growth mindset was a Grade 5 student building a trebuchet in a timed building competition. She had decided on a design that she thought would be great and started to build it. Every time she tested it, it would slingshot the arm up and over the base, hit a cross-section on the top, drop the ball directly in front of the trebuchet, and completely smash the entire base. This happened repeatedly. Her growth mindset had her in a position of "I can" thinking, and she became so locked on that design idea that she wasn't able to give herself permission to abandon her plan, be creative, and try something new. In the end, she ran out of time, didn't complete the challenge, and left feeling deflated. As Hattie says, a growth mindset "may not help if it leads to more practice on a task using already failed strategies, and seeking experts to provide alternative strategies may be more effective than believing that 'I can' and other growth notions" (Hazell, 2017, para. 11).

What is a Flexible Mindset?

The bridge between a growth mindset and a fixed mindset is a flexible mindset. It requires a learner to be reflective, recognize when they are thinking in a fixed manner, and figure out how to move towards a growth mindset. This is often necessary when you don't know where to start on a task, struggle to find an answer, fail repeatedly, or are nervous about the outcome of a decision. The flexible mindset offers an intricate balance between seeking out learning opportunities that will stretch the mind versus overwhelming oneself and being stuck in a fixed mindset for too long. In the case of the student repeatedly failing at building a working trebuchet, a flexible mindset would have suggested trying a new design. This approach sometimes needs to be taught and needs practice by having an adult or peer give feedback and ask questions like, "I wonder what would happen if we made the base stronger?" Similar to physical flexibility, a flexible mindset requires challenging the mind to go beyond its typical range of motion. A flexible mindset can lead to better problem-solving, enhanced creativity, and less suffering after a setback.

When one of the teams I was working with was collecting data with the goal of improving student success, I saw the benefits of having a flexible mindset up close and personal. We were going through the mundane task of administering certain agreed-upon assessments, recording the results on a class list, and sharing the data once a month at our divisional meeting. We had established a fixed routine, confident that there was no need to change our current practices. At one of these meetings I started to wonder how we could more efficiently share data with each other to work more collaboratively and be more responsive to our students' needs. I didn't have an answer, wasn't sure where to start, and wasn't sure if the result was going to be better or worse; however, I was willing to try. I began to ask questions of my professional learning team (PLT), and then I started playing around with different spreadsheets and ideas. Along the way, I made a few mistakes and lost a large chunk of data. At that point, it would have been easy simply to go back to our established ways of thinking and doing things. Fortunately, I persisted. Having a flexible mindset helped me to persevere with an open mind, and I found a way to collect data, comment on it, add pictures, capture audio, and share this information in a way that any educator working with these children could access and add to. This flexible mindset led to a growth mindset as we continued to build upon this new methodology and co-create ability groups from different classes based on this new way of collecting data. I encourage you to develop mental flexibility by overriding your fixed mindset, changing your mental perceptions, and implementing new exercises.

Promoting Flexible and Growth Mindsets

By actively advocating for both flexible and growth mindsets — and also explaining when a fixed mindset might work better — we allow students to understand and practice when to exercise each. As educators, promoting flexible and growth mindsets within ourselves prepares us to try new approaches in our classroom. We can then make sure that students become better equipped to tackle problems and to think deeply about how they are thinking (metacognition). Learning more about their thinking processes will help us further in teaching ideas and strategies that students can utilize. The possibilities for growth are endless.

Paul Chernyak, a Licensed Professional Counselor, provides several great ideas to help you achieve a flexible mindset. Here are some of them, and we will examine these ones in more detail below:

1. Watch Out for Being Closed-Minded
2. Less Defence, More Offence
3. Praise Effort Over Skill
4. Embrace Criticism
5. Curiosity Grows the Brain
6. Embrace the Challenge
7. Positive Self-Talk
8. One Step Back, but Two Steps Forward
9. Change Your Routine

1. Watch Out for Being Closed-Minded

People who are closed-minded have a hard time looking at life through an asset-based lens to see what they are capable of. You may be thinking this way if you find yourself constantly saying that something won't work, that there are no solutions to issues, or if you get frustrated with the successful people around you. You may feel maxed out in your ability to contribute meaningful ideas to conversations, you may feel deflated, or that your ability to impact change is stunted. At times, it may be hard to notice these characteristics within yourself when you are stuck in a closed-minded state. To avoid slipping into this mindset, have a friend, family member, or colleague observe your body language in group environments and record verbatim what you say. This prevents bias and allows you to reflect on your words as they were written down. This will help you to become reflective and honest with yourself to notice when you are slipping into a closed mindset (Chernyak, n.d., method 1, item 1).

2. Less Defence, More Offence

Do you find yourself being defensive if your views aren't popular or if someone challenges your opinions? This may be a normal part of human nature, but if we don't challenge our own perceptions of how others view us, we run the risk of putting people off with our defensiveness. We must promote flexibility by stretching our thoughts and emotions beyond what we think we are capable of. When we turn defensiveness into offensively challenging our own belief systems, then we can grow. This can be done by recording a conversation (with permission of those around you) to analyze the language you are using. Language such as "We can't...," "I don't think...," and "I doubt we can..." need to be replaced with "Not yet...," "Could we...?," or "Perhaps if..." Coach yourself through this positivity lens to promote growth. With a *growth mindset* as the focus, this is a great exercise to model, and to *do* with students when teaching learning skills, especially organization and problem solving. Give them permission to "park" something less important and tackle the tough task right away (Chernyak, n.d., method 1, item 2).

3. Praise Effort Over Skill

Skills seem to be something that many people believe we are born with; those with a fixed mindset believe that either you have skill or you don't. We run the risk of stunting our self-esteem and creativity because we think it's not possible anyways, so why bother trying? For years, I refused to play pick-up basketball with my friends because I thought I didn't naturally have the skill set or talent to play. This fixed mindset inevitably made me miss out on a lot of fun, but it also forced me to avoid taking on challenges. I finally reflected on why I didn't want to play and found that my inflexibility in thinking made me believe that I couldn't marry skill with effort. I didn't understand that they work simultaneously. By being reflective, we may be able to recognize how our effort can positively impact our outcomes. Here are some examples of approaches you could take with your students:

- "I can tell you worked hard on that."
- "You must be proud of your effort on that."
- "I really like the detail you used."
- "What do you like best about your effort?" (Chernyak, n.d., method 1, item 3)

4. Embrace Criticism

Feedback is critical to becoming better at what we do. In a fixed mindset, feedback and criticism become a shot to the ego, a personal attack on our pride, and a shattering hit to our self-esteem. This happened to me when someone suggested that I move around too much during presentations, making the audience seasick and unable to absorb my message because they were distracted by my body language. I fluffed it off, thinking my critic was out of their mind. It wasn't until I saw myself on video that I had to admit it was true. With a flexible state of mind, we can ask for feedback so that we can learn and improve. By not taking it personally, we open ourselves to the opportunity for growth. Take the time to ask your students if they understood what you taught. If they say no, ask what specifically they didn't understand — and ask them if they have any suggestions about what would make it easier for them to understand (Chernyak, n.d., method 1, item 4).

5. Curiosity Grows the Brain

Curiosity is a natural part of our human nature. Just like animals, at a young age we are naturally curious about the world around us. What is that? What does this do? How does that work? How is that made? Why does that work? A person with an open mind keeps asking authentic questions. When we think in a fixed manner, our curiosity diminishes and we are less likely to care or want to know the outcome.

As we lose our desire to ask questions, we engage less with the world around us. To avoid this, encourage a childlike approach to teaching and learning concepts both old and new. Imagine the negative impact on learning if our students lost their curiosity. In order to promote a growth mindset, ask your students about a new game they are curious about or a video game that they are interested in. Ask them why they like it, how it works, what would happen if…? Model the natural curiosity that you aspire to see in them (Chernyak, n.d., method 2, item 1).

6. Embrace the Challenge

Face challenges head on and don't allow yourself to pass them off to someone else. In a fixed mindset, we see challenges as obstacles that we can't surmount, almost as if they deliberately get in our way. Rather than allowing these obstacles to compound, start by reflecting on the events leading up the challenge. Think about how it was handled and what the outcome was. This will allow you to think flexibly about what you could do differently to better handle the next challenge. Add this new idea to your problem-solving tool kit. Now start embracing one challenge at a time so you can practice this new skill. This will move you towards a growth mindset, promoting creative thinking to activate problem-solving skills for similar challenges in the future. See yourself as adept at handling difficulties and soon you will be calling problems by a new name — opportunities. Ask students how they would solve a particular problem if they were the teacher. This will help them move beyond thinking about themselves and move them into the shoes of an outsider who can help them (Chernyak, n.d., method 2, item 2).

7. Positive Self-Talk

Your inner dialogue is one of your most powerful tools. The brain can work with you or against you. You must choose how to leverage its power in your favour. The fixed mindset suppresses you into thinking that you aren't capable of achieving, that others are better than you, and that you don't have what it takes to be successful. To avoid these negative thoughts, list all of your positive qualities and the positive feedback you receive from others. Read the list periodically or post it where you can see it regularly. Another option when you need to use positive self-talk is to journal. The more you can repeat these reminders, the more you will believe them. Have students create a personalized list of affirmative comments so they have some tools to use in tough situations when positive inner dialogue would help them persist (Chernyak, n.d., method 2, item 2).

8. One Step Back, but Two Steps Forward

If at first you don't succeed, try, try again. As my parents would say, "If you fall off the horse, get right back on." This positive way of thinking allows you to persist despite setbacks, which are simply reminders that you are learning. Without setbacks, you are only reviewing, not learning something new. Allow setbacks to flow in and out of your journey and remind yourself that they are healthy opportunities for growth rather than blows against your goals. Mastering a new tech tool by the end of the year is not necessary. What is necessary is to keep exploring tech, as you will learn many new skills you wouldn't have otherwise. Now identify what prevented you from achieving mastery and thank the obstacles that got in your way because they allowed you to learn other important information. Do this with your students as well. Ask them to reflect on something that that didn't go well or that they failed to achieve. Support them by asking what would have made the outcome better and encourage them to apply this new strategy next time around (Chernyak, n.d., method 2, item 3).

9. Change Your Routine

Get out of that comfort zone! Structure and routine help you feel safe but do nothing for mental flexibility. Start with slight tweaks to your normal routine. If you typically jump straight into your lesson delivery, try starting with an exercise instead. Use an exit slip on the way out with three reflective questions for students to think about to extend their learning. Ask a colleague for a different way to assess an upcoming task. Switch things up. You can help students by allowing them to take mindful breaks, like a seventh inning stretch, to allow them to decompress and refocus throughout the lesson (Chernyak, n.d., method 3, item 4).

These ideas can help you achieve flexible and growth mindsets with the overarching goal of making you better able to teach students to do the same. Teachers must provide rich tasks for students to struggle with and persevere while modelling a flexible mindset by making mistakes and working through them publicly. Educational Assistants (EAs) need to coach struggling students to apply the strategies they have been taught, resisting the urge to do everything for them. Administrators need to model making mistakes — and admitting to failures — to gain trust and respect as well as to demonstrate flexible thinking. I have found several useful ways to model to students how to move towards a flexible/growth mindset, which we will look at next.

Failure Has Benefits

Psychologist Jason Moser studied the neural mechanisms that operate in people's brains when they make mistakes. Moser and his group found something fascinating. When we make a mistake, synapses fire. A synapse is an electrical signal that moves between parts of the brain when learning occurs.

> When people make a mistake, the brain has two potential responses. The first, called an ERN response, is increased electrical activity that is thought to occur when the brain experiences conflict between a correct response and an error. Interestingly, this brain activity occurs whether or not the person making the response knows they have made an error. The second response, called a Pe, is a brain signal thought to reflect conscious attention to mistakes. This happens when there is awareness that an error has been made and conscious attention is paid to the error. (Moser, Schroder, Heeter, Moran, & Lee, 2011, para. 1–2)

For instance, a mathematician takes a math problem as a challenge, and with that challenge often comes failure. They look at it from many different perspectives to understand why one approach didn't work.

That analysis of their failure (usually many failures along the way) leads to true understanding when they get it right. Thomas A. Edison once said, "I have not failed. I've just found 10,000 ways that won't work." It's critical that we promote failures as opportunities to enrich learning, not see them as barriers that can leave students feeling incapable.

Overcoming Perceived Threats

Educators often declare themselves as having a growth mindset, but it is not that simple. Achieving an overall growth mindset is a life-time journey, and growth must be nurtured. Every one of us is a mixture of all three mindsets; sometimes we're in a growth mindset, sometimes we can bridge them (flexible mindset), and sometimes we're triggered into a fixed mindset by what we perceive as threats. Challenges, mistakes, failures, or criticisms can threaten our sense of our own abilities. Venturing into unknown territory with a new teaching method, confronting a student who is not learning, or comparing ourselves to someone we perceive to be a more accomplished educator are examples many educators will be familiar with. All too often we are stuck teaching the same way we've always done it because it's safe and easy, but it doesn't always mean it's working — and that is certainly not indicative of a growth mindset.

In order to work toward a more flexible, growth-oriented mindset, we need to observe ourselves and find our triggers. Spend several weeks noticing when you enter a more threatened, defensive state. Don't judge yourself. Don't fight it. Just observe. Susan Mackie, a colleague of Carol Dweck, advises that you give your fixed-mindset persona a name. Talk to it; call it by name when it shows up. Over time, try to recruit it into collaborating on your goals instead of letting it undermine you with doubts and fears (Dweck, 2016, para. 13). Dweck warns us about confusing a growth mindset with a false-growth mindset, as effort alone does not lead to growth. According to Dweck,

Great effort has become the consolation prize for children who weren't learning. So the very students who most needed to learn about developing their abilities were instead receiving praise for their ineffective effort. Instead educators and parents should praise students' process (their hard work, strategies, focus, and persistence) and tie it to their performance, learning, goals, and progress. Teachers need to tell the truth. They can acknowledge laudable effort, but they also need to acknowledge when students are not learning effectively, and then work with them to find new learning strategies (2016, para. 6).

Remember, the goal is to nurture an adaptable mindset — one suitable for navigating a confusing, chaotic world — in which we see failure as an opportunity to grow.

Grit versus Resilience

According to Angela Duckworth, whose 2013 TED talk on grit has over 15 million views, grit means "perseverance and passion for long-term goals."[2] It is fascinating how individuals with similar levels of education, access to resources, and ability have varying degrees of success when setting out to achieve long-term goals. The ability to push on over a long period requires maintaining a high level of motivation, dedication, and a passion for the goal itself. Resilience, on the other hand, involves the ability to pick yourself up after failing and respond more assertively in subsequent attempts. So how are they different?

The subtle difference between these two deeply entwined character traits seems to be that **resilience** means having the optimism to continue when times are tough and you've experienced some failures, when

---

2   https://www.ted.com/talks/
    angela_lee_duckworth_grit_the_power_of_passion_and_perseverance?language=en

others see continuing as futile or impossible. **Grit** is the drive that keeps you on a difficult task over a sustained period of time (Lechner, 2018, para. 4). Roger Clemens, a potential future Major League Baseball Hall-of-Fame pitcher, once said in an interview, "Most kids in Double-A ball have the skill to play in the big leagues, they just can't handle the high level of failure they experience over time." Even one of the best pitchers ever, over the course of his 24-year career,[3] won only 65.8% of the time — a good example of both resilience and grit.

The good news is that you can change your mindset, which can also increase your grit. According to Dweck, Walton, and Cohen (2014), tenacity and its effects on achievement, especially in an educational setting, are affected by the following factors:

- Beliefs about oneself
- Goals
- Feelings about social connectedness
- Self-regulatory skills

When students have a growth mindset, they respond to adversity and failure with constructive thoughts, and their behaviour shows persistence and resilience. If we develop grit, failure no longer makes us afraid to try something new. In her 2018 article *Resilience and Grit: How to Develop a Growth Mindset*, Tamara Lechner provides five tips for you and your students to develop grit and resilience:

1. Choose Your Words Wisely

The words you choose when giving praise can affect people's resilience and mindset. If we simply praise the skill a person has, then we imply that someone either has that skill or they don't, ultimately reinforcing the idea that skill is a static attribute. If we say, for example, "Wow, you are really smart. You are excellent at that," we aren't giving credit for the effort put forth or the process of planning and thinking their way through a task. Instead, we can praise the effort to reinforce the idea that skills can be developed and acquired and that learning isn't

---

3   https://www.mlb.com/player/roger-clemens-112388

static. Comments like, "I can tell you worked really hard to finish that," or "You must have put a lot of thought into that; tell me about how you planned that out," acknowledge not just the skill but also its current application. Recognizing and promoting effort or strategy promotes resilience by allowing students to understand that thinking is flexible and multidimensional. This allows them to move towards a flexible mindset by promoting an approach that affirms that skill plus effort can equal success (Lechner, 2018, para. 9).

2. Positive Circle of Influence

Surround yourself with positive people and good things will happen. If we regularly think positive thoughts and act in positive ways, positivity becomes part of our character. Not only does it become the way you carry yourself each day, it also becomes infectious. The opposite also holds true. If you are constantly surrounded by negativity, it too becomes your default position of thinking and acting. I always remind my students to be aware of who they surround themselves with and to make positive choices. If we expect our students to do this, isn't it time we adults do the same? Are you one of those pessimistic people at staff meetings or professional development sessions? Or are you open to new ideas, optimistic that one of them might work in your favour? (Lechner, 2018, para. 10).

3. Default to Flexibility

People who are flexible in their thinking see problems as unsolved mysteries. They turn problems into opportunities to express their creative-thinking skills and accept that barrier as a challenge. This confidence starts to promote resilience and eventually increases their grit. As people creatively solve one problem after another, they increase their willingness to try something new and make mistakes (Lechner, 2018, para. 11).

4. Promote Your Moral Purpose

People who share and model their moral purpose create an environment where everyone is working to achieve a common goal. Be clear about what your purpose is and set short-term goals to achieve it. By doing this, you help those around you to align their focus with yours, which is a natural leadership technique (Lechner, 2018, para. 12).

5. Reflection Time

People who take time to reflect in a non-judgemental way are better equipped to deal with adverse situations because they have already thought through what worked and what didn't. This promotes self-learning, allowing them to better prepare for similar situations in the future. Being reflective is part of a flexible mindset because it allows you to recalibrate when necessary (Lechner, 2108, para. 13).

Like most valuable skills, resilience and grit take practice, says Lechner. However, the work is well worth the effort, because fostering these mindset-expanding traits will have a positive impact on every aspect of your life (Lechner, 2018, para. 14). While these are all practical strategies for adults, we can also coach our students to use them in order to move forward constructively. Dweck (2016) suggests that it is the educator's task to create a growth mindset classroom. In the safety of these classrooms, students can begin to leave behind their fixed mindsets and develop a willingness to try to be okay with failing rather than failing to try.

What Can Educators Do?

Provide meaningful work: Both my current and previous school provide students with opportunities to do action research to determine a need for a product to improve society. Involve the community, design something, and pitch the idea to them. Build the prototype, market it, and sell it. This type of project could incorporate multiple areas of a curriculum, allowing students to think and express themselves in many different ways. It also allows the educator to assess a variety of tasks in a variety of ways. Another interesting approach is to host a manufacturing night. This requires students to design and build items that they will sell to the community. I have helped several schools set these up. The students love it because it has an element of friendly competitiveness, and failure is ongoing and safe. They are invested in it because they are picking a product that they believe will sell. They also decide what charity or organization to donate the funds they raise to. This is a great way to involve the community, create excitement at the school, and give a meaningful reason for parents to donate money to a good cause.

Offer honest and helpful feedback: "I really like how you hooked my attention with your topic sentence, but your supporting sentences lack enough specific information to support the main idea. Please include one more specific detail in the second and third sentence using your success criteria for writing a solid supporting sentence."

Share advice on future learning strategies: If a student is efficient at skip-counting by 5's, suggest that the next step is to try multiplication using groups of 5 to become even more efficient.

Create opportunities to revise their work and show their learning: Build in reflective time during the day for students to improve their work. This might be a centre in your literacy block; it might be during 1:1 conferencing with you, or in a small, guided group with common opportunities for students to reflect. Have them log or record this process as part of their — and your — assessment and documentation. It's also a nice opportunity to share and demonstrate to parents how their child is progressing.

Ideas to try with colleagues or in the classroom

What risks have you taken in your professional career in the last month?

What risks are you willing to take next month?

Determine an area in your teaching practice towards which you have a fixed mindset. Write it down. Decide on two strategies from this chapter that will help you exercise flexibility in your thinking to help you move closer to a growth mindset. Reflect on your initial thoughts in two months and record what allowed you to shift your thinking or what prevented you from doing so. Remember, we learn just as much from what didn't work as what did.

Chapter 3

Failing Through Barriers:
How Students Succeed

*A life spent making mistakes is not only more honourable
but more useful than a life spent in doing nothing.*
                                        —George Bernard Shaw

Throughout this chapter, we will look into planning for our marginalized students, and begin to relate to their struggles so we can best support them as educators. Often, we plan amazing lessons and units with the entire class in mind. This seems like a natural way to plan what we are going to do; after all, we must reach every child in our class — and ultimately in our schools. However, "planning for the entire class" usually means planning for the whole class *all at once*, not in a way that accounts for all different types, levels, and learning styles of students in a *multiple-parts-of-the-class* way. Are we being intentional in our planning? Are we prioritizing our marginalized students? The majority of our students will likely learn the content with few setbacks or major failures. Can the same be said of our students with IEPs, our English Language Learners (ELLs), our students struggling with their identity, or our students living well below the poverty line?

This chapter is about prioritizing students flagged as potentially at risk of not succeeding *without specific, intentional planning* to help them achieve the best they can. Once we begin our planning, assessment, and curriculum delivery with these students in mind, we start to see prolific gains in our entire classroom and school culture. We start to see other students recognize these students as capable and competent contributing members of the school body. No longer are they seen as marginalized because, perhaps for the first time, they truly aren't. The reason they were labelled as "marginalized" is simply societal perceptions and beliefs. We need our education system to redefine those perceptions; we need to move from a negative lens to a positive one. This shift is required in every education system, so I hope to provide you with some new ideas and strategies as you work through this chapter.

When I Learned to Fail: French Immersion

I was enrolled in Ontario's French Immersion (FI) program from Kindergarten through Grade 12, and in a constant state of disequilibrium and cognitive dissonance. Daily, I was faced with new words in new contexts. At times, it was overwhelming and frustrating to the point where I wanted to quit. I thought it would be so much easier in the English stream since there wouldn't be as many barriers to overcome in order to learn new concepts. Although this was likely true, I'm so glad I didn't choose the "easy" road. I believe adversity — along with a relatively safe environment for failure (which thankfully my parents provided) — at an early age promotes grit, perseverance, and determination. Without even knowing it, I was overcoming adversity on a regular basis and learning how to fail.

My parents' support and encouragement helped me advance to the point that, at the age of eight, I was able to speak with transportation drivers from Quebec to help make our family business more successful. Every weekend I faced the astronomical pressure of knowing that I might fail to communicate accurately in French, and expensive loads of livestock might not show up on time to our family farm. It took a great deal of perseverance to use broken French with some English thrown in to coordinate these business transactions, but it provided invaluable real-life experience. Needing to apply my French-language education in a meaningful context outside of school helped me deal with the adversity of learning a new language. It helped me overcome my fear of failure. Such authentic opportunities and experiences need to be part of the school day rather than one-off activities to show mastery at the end of an otherwise abstract approach.

Although I stuck it out, Canadian Parents for French (CPF) reports that 5,309 students graduated in 2016 with a Grade 12 FI credit, representing 42% of the original Grade 1 cohort with a small influx of middle- and late-immersion students. In Core French, 8,952 students graduated with a Grade 12 credit in 2011–2012, representing 7% of the original Grade 4 cohort in 2003–2004. Of all Grade 12 students in the English school boards, 7% take a Grade 12 FSL course (Core, Extended or Immersion; Canadian Parents for French, 2019, p. 2).[4] Attrition has been an ongoing issue for French Immersion for years, possibly because there are only two entry points (Kindergarten registration and late immersion) but many possible exit points (i.e., at the end of every school year). Unfortunately, there are also teachers and schools that believe French Immersion is elitist and only for the academically advanced. This can result in fewer children, or parents, being encouraged to take that route. Another challenge is that by beginning French Immersion in Junior Kindergarten (JK) you are dealing with extremely active children. Without clear communication — they don't know French yet and English isn't spoken — it can create even more issues.

This was the case when I, and then two years later my twin brothers, showed up. We were three young students with endless amounts of energy and not much interest in school. Keeping our interest when we would rather be out chasing cows around the field or playing road hockey became extra difficult for the teacher when we couldn't easily understand what was being said. I began in Kindergarten, and not being able to read in English while my non-French-Immersion friends could was embarrassing. I constantly felt behind and very much like a failure. Learning math concepts in French was also a struggle, particularly because I didn't know some of the key mathematical terminology in English either. My parents didn't speak any French, a situation many people who put their children in French Immersion will understand,

---

4   Source for all Ontario statistics: Enrolment figures as reported by schools in the Ontario School Information System (OnSYS), October 2015-2016 and earlier years for comparison purposes, Ministry of Education.

so for them to support me in all subject areas became increasingly difficult, especially in later grades. For example, in Grade 10 math my final grade was 50%. This was partly due to the effort required to think in both languages, and was exacerbated by having learned all of these foundational concepts in French in my early years but being taught in English in the later years. It also had to do with the environment and curriculum delivery that was not suitable for a learner like me. In my case, I'm sure that I would have benefited from an Individual Education Plan (IEP) to better access educational content and processes.

With my 50% in that math class, I was enrollment in summer school. Although I was initially hesitant — after all, it involved a 45-minute bus ride each way, then class from 9 am to 12 noon Monday to Friday for three weeks — something had changed for me. I was beginning to realizing that my past failures were in fact creating opportunities for me. For example, I was beginning to think of French as a potential opportunity to increase my chances of getting a job. After all, I had been helping my dad communicate with French cattle-truck drivers since I was eight. By Grade 10, I was negotiating business deals for significant amounts of money. This real-world application provided an incentive to keep learning French. The second thing that started to change my opinions about school as a pathway in life was my potential for scholarships. While I wasn't your typical sit-still A+ student, I was always thinking through a business and entrepreneurial lens, so the thought of free university only made sense. I had the good fortune to be selected onto a few all-star teams for baseball, and we played in some big tournaments. These tournaments brought out scouts, which meant opportunity. At the same time, I had set a few track and field records in the 110 metre and 400 metre hurdles. This meant a chance to compete at provincial-level meets, facing the best competition around — this also created opportunity. These opportunities also meant high expectations academically. In addition to my sport-specific stats, scouts and coaches wanted to know my marks! This provided the motivation for me to achieve 88% at summer school and graduate at the end of Grade 10 with a 79% overall average. I just missed being on the honour role, but best of all was that I figured out how to make the system work for me.

Upon graduating Grade 12 with my Diplome d'Étude en Immersion, I was offered six scholarships. I failed my way to success.

I was not alone in the ability to overcome adversity and a fear of failure. In both French Immersion and English-as-a-Second-Language (ESL) programs, students are attempting to acquire a new language in a foreign environment. Failure is a constant, yet so too is overcoming adversity. How is it that these children are able to succeed? Where do they get the perseverance and determination to continue through challenging daily activities and tests? Who taught them to keep taking risks? What are those teachers doing to pique their interest and curiosity, encouraging them to become comfortable with failure, day after day after day?

What about students with specialized learning needs? They display incredible willpower in continuing to push the education system to become more flexible and to allow them the same opportunities. Learning to fail productively means learning to show society what assets they are to the community. Often the barriers — human, political, and environmental — are so great that these students have been forced into a deficit model where failure is almost inevitable. Where did they learn that quitting isn't an option? How do they intrinsically recognize and take advantage of opportunities to succeed as motivation to excel and improve? As one student put it, "I just want to be as good as everybody else and that means I have to work hard every day!" Failing along the way is to be expected, so let's learn to embrace it.

English Language Learners

Imagine the daily grind and extra brainpower required to learn the entire spectrum of subject areas while being an ESL student. Let's look at some mathematical examples to highlight how students who are learning another language — and come from another country or culture — have to face adversity on a regular basis:

- Decimal point and commas vary from culture to culture. Depending on the location of a comma or decimal point, the mathematical meaning can change drastically. For example, $300.50 in English is 300,50$ in French.

- Opinions about rote memory versus process-based answers vary from culture to culture. Students from other countries may be focused solely on the correct response and may not be able to justify their answer. In Canada, on the other hand, we are very process-focused *as well as* wanting the correct response.
- Students may never have seen or used manipulatives and may find them challenging to use if they are not taught explicitly how to incorporate them into their schema.
- Often specific mathematical terminology doesn't translate accurately from one language to the next.

With all these built-in challenges for certain students, it is crucial for them to be able to demonstrate their struggles, and the differences from country to country. This would allow all students to understand that they are not alone in dealing with failure. Imagine a student struggling with a concept who learns that other students are also struggling. Imagine how powerful it would be when they realize they can overcome adversity together, gaining critical knowledge through facing these difficulties. When I interviewed a range of students (Kindergarten to Grade 8) from Pakistan, Syria, Portugal, Nepal, Iran, Iraq, India, and Nigeria, I asked what they thought it meant to be a "failure." Every one of them referred to either poor grades in school or not being good at a game, like soccer. The most common response from students in Grades 3 to 8 was about not achieving well in school. The more common outlook from the younger students, Kindergarten to Grade 3, was that it meant you aren't good at something right now, but you could improve. I found it interesting that many of the students in older grades prefaced their comments with, "according to adults." The most fascinating part of my conversations was that each student told me that even though you might not be good at something, or that you have not achieved a high mark, grade, or standard, you can still work towards getting better. In other words, they still believed in *learning*. To me, this speaks about the power of "yet." It suggests that the negative association with failure is not culturally based nor age related, but instead may be more environmentally based. When students — and adults — are surrounded by people with a positive, flexible mindset, it follows that they would be more productive and willing to accept failure and adversity as part of a learning journey.

Although newcomers desperately want to "fit in" and adopt the new language, it is critical to value and encourage a student's first language (L1). Students with well-developed skills in their first language have been shown to acquire an additional language more easily and fully, which has a positive impact on academic achievement (Genesee, Lindholm-Leary, Saunders, & Christian, 2006, p. 69). If schools and teachers aren't honouring this, we are actively failing these students and their future language-development endeavours. We need to encourage English-language learners to maintain and develop their own languages because the ability to speak more than one language is an asset to the individual, the community, and the nation (Coelho, 2004, p. 9). We need to allow them to fail, try again, fail again, and still be proud of their efforts.

It's also important to recognize that English-language learners typically develop basic oral communication skills (BOCS) and conversational fluency over the span of one to two years (Ontario Ministry of Education, 2005, p. 49). It takes five to seven years for ESL students to develop the academic English proficiency and Cognitive Academic Language Proficiency (CALP) needed to express and explore curriculum concepts (Ontario Ministry of Education, 2008, p. 12). Students who have no or limited first language literacy (ELD profile) will often need more time than most English-language learners to develop academic English proficiency (Ontario Ministry of Education, 2008, p. 5). It may take them ten years or longer to catch up to their peers (Coelho, 2004, p. 152). With all this built-in challenge facing them every day, these students are excellent examples of knowing how to fail toward success.

What Can Teachers/Educators Do?

It is critical for teachers to know this information, and then take up their responsibility to plan and assess accordingly. The Ontario Ministry of Education has released a document called STEP (Steps to English Proficiency). I had the good fortune of contributing to this document, which is a sound resource in supporting language acquisition for a range of learners. It includes continua for Kindergarten, Grades 1–3, 4–6, 7–8, and 9–12. On top of the initial assessment intended for classroom teachers to use, there are also Observable Language Behaviours (OLBs) as part of ongoing assessments. Within each are the necessary elements required to learn reading, writing, and oral communication. Below is an example of each of the primary (Grades 1–3) OLBs:

Reading

Element	Observable Language Behaviours (OLB)					
	Step 1	Step 2	Step 3	Step 4	Step 5	Step 6
Meaning Understand and respond to texts, using strategies	Demonstrate understanding by responding to a highly visual text, using a combination of visuals, drawings, L1, pre-taught vocabulary and non-verbal cues Read and follow simply worded instructions with visual support Recognize patterns in text, directionality of print and the letters of his/her name	Demonstrate understanding by responding to a visual text, using drawings, L1, pre-taught vocabulary and high frequency words Read and follow short, simply worded instructions Recognize simple patterns in text and most upper and lower case letters of the alphabet	Demonstrate understanding by responding to a simple or adapted text supported by visuals Read and follow instructions consisting of a few simple steps for an authentic task Recognize patterns in text, upper and lower case letters and some sound/symbol patterns	Demonstrate understanding by responding to authentic texts with linguistic complexity approaching grade level Read and follow instructions consisting of multiple steps for an authentic task	Demonstrate understanding by responding to authentic texts, from a variety of genres, with the linguistic complexity of early grade level Read and follow instructions consisting of multiple steps for a variety of tasks	Demonstrate understanding by responding to a wide variety of grade-appropriate text with vocabulary support
Form and Style Use text features, text forms and style to construct meaning	Locate information in a highly visual text, using visual cues and pre-taught vocabulary	Locate information in a text, using visual cues and pre-taught vocabulary	Identify and use common text features to locate information	Identify and use a variety of text features to locate information	Identify text features and explain how they help readers understand text	Identify different text forms and features and explain how they help readers understand the text
Fluency Read and understand familiar and unfamiliar words and phrases, and expand vocabulary	Read and understand personally relevant words, using visuals and sound-symbol connections	Read and understand high frequency words and pre-taught vocabulary in context Decode unfamiliar vocabulary supported by key visuals	Read and understand key pre-taught academic words Decode unfamiliar vocabulary, using key visuals and other cueing systems	Read and understand high-frequency words and phrases and key academic vocabulary Determine meaning of some unfamiliar words, using some cueing systems	Read and understand low frequency words, phrases and academic vocabulary Determine meaning of unfamiliar words, using context, sentence structure and sound-symbol patterns	Read and understand most vocabulary in grade-appropriate texts Consistently use a variety of strategies to solve unfamiliar words

Source: STEP (Steps to English Proficiency), Ontario Ministry of Education.

Writing

Element	Observable Language Behaviours (OLB)					
	Step 1	Step 2	Step 3	Step 4	Step 5	Step 6
Developing and Organizing Content						
Engage in prewriting to generate ideas and information	Generate key ideas using L1, English, and/or visuals by answering simple questions about personal experiences	Generate ideas by brainstorming with peers and teachers in L1 and English about personally relevant topics	Generate ideas with peers, using familiar strategies	Generate ideas about a topic, using a variety of strategies and key academic vocabulary	Generate ideas, using a variety of strategies and resources and academic vocabulary	Locate and select information for a writing topic, using resources
Organize ideas and information	Organize key information, using visuals, single words and phrases, and L1 with a teacher-generated model	Organize ideas and/or key information, using visuals, L1 and English with a teacher-generated model	Sort and organize ideas or key information into teacher-selected categories	Sort and organize ideas and information, using a teacher-selected strategy	Sort and organize ideas and information, using a self-selected strategy	Sort and organize ideas and information, using an effective and efficient strategy
Form and Style						
Incorporate a variety of text forms and features in writing	Participate in a shared writing activity using personally relevant English words and L1	Write using a combination of pictures and familiar words	Write simple sentences using familiar words and a framework provided by the teacher	Write about a familiar topic, using linked sentences and a specific text form	Write simple texts in a form appropriate to the writing purpose	Identify and use text features and forms appropriate for specific writing purposes
Language Conventions						
Choose words that convey specific meaning and add interest to the writing	Select appropriate words from a list with visual support, using English and L1	Select appropriate high-frequency words and familiar vocabulary to write about a personally relevant topic	Choose key subject-specific words to write about a topic	Choose expressive and subject-specific vocabulary to write in a variety of forms	Choose academic vocabulary to write for a specific purpose. Use some low-frequency words	Choose vocabulary that includes innovative and expressive language to engage the reader
Write with fluency using a variety of sentence structures	Write simple sentences following a model provided by the teacher	Write simple sentences	Write simple compound sentences	Write a variety of simple and compound sentences	Write a variety of linked simple and compound sentences	Write a variety of simple sentences to elaborate ideas and enhance meaning

Source: STEP (Steps to English Proficiency), Ontario Ministry of Education.

Oral Communication

Element	Observable Language Behaviours (OLB)					
	Step 1	**Step 2**	**Step 3**	**Step 4**	**Step 5**	**Step 6**
Listening						
Listen and respond for a variety of purposes	Respond to personally relevant questions with gestures, and L1 interspersed with English words and phrases Follow simple instructions for classroom routines, using visual cues and pre-taught English words and phrases	Respond to simple questions with single words or phrases in English, and L1 Follow simple instructions	Listen to an oral text and demonstrate understanding through active participation Follow multi-step instructions	Respond to an oral text by identifying key information with teacher prompts	Respond to oral texts on grade-level topics with vocabulary and grammar support	Respond to an oral academic text through active participation in a class discussion with some vocabulary and grammar support
Speaking						
Use vocabulary and other language features in a comprehensible and grammatically accurate way	Use familiar words to express meaning Express personal needs using gestures, and L1 interspersed with English words and phrases	Use pre-taught vocabulary in simple sentences Use simple conjunctions to join words and phrases in speech	Use high frequency words in appropriate context Use compound sentences in speech	Use high and low frequency words in appropriate context Use a teacher-selected grammatical structure to increase speaking accuracy and clarity	Use an expanded range of vocabulary to participate in classroom discussions Use a range of grammatical structures to increase speaking accuracy and clarity	Select a range of social and academic vocabulary to enhance meaning using a range of grammatical structures
Use language strategically to communicate for a variety of purposes	Use non-verbal communication to convey and receive messages Use gestures, key words, phrases and L1 to identify items	Use a small range of personal words and phrases to make and respond to requests in familiar situations Participate in social interactions with peers, using English and L1	Participate with some prompting in academic discussions using short phrases and sentences Initiate and engage in social interactions with peers using familiar vocabulary	Use subject-specific language to state an opinion Begin to self-correct simple grammatical errors	Use language to effectively share ideas and opinions Speak with fluency and clarity in group situations	Use most language structures appropriate to the grade level

Source: STEP (Steps to English Proficiency), Ontario Ministry of Education.

Teachers need to be open to asking for support in working with this document. It is not acceptable to plan whole-class lessons and expect learning to happen through osmosis. We are actively failing our students if we do this. Some learning will occur simply through exposure, but that's not good enough. Throughout my five years as a curriculum consultant for ESL, I would often show up at schools to help support student learning only to find the non-English-speaking students off in a corner listening to some online software that claims to teach English. Although these programs have a place in supporting ongoing language acquisition, we cannot replace the invaluable face-to-face interactions of a human teacher. I am a huge supporter of using technology to support learning, but it will never replace good teaching. Ask yourself, why *this* program for *this* child at *this* time? If the reason is that you don't know what else to do with this student at this time, then we have all failed that student. We need to be willing to ask for support, just as we encourage our students to do. Educators need to become more comfortable in understanding and modelling for students how failure can lead to success.

So how can we empower ELLs in our current system to continue taking the risks required to learn a new language while supporting their first language? Here are some suggestions based on my experience:

- **Begin planning every unit and lesson with them in mind.** Put your highest need students at the centre of a circular diagram. Use their names so they are present with you all the time as you plan. Start to layer all the expectations and outcomes around them, and ask yourself, "Are these students going to have an entry point?" If the answer is no, then be creative about how they could access those outcomes. Lean on your resource teacher, administrator, board level supports, and the students' families for ideas to empower them to be successful. If you plan for ELL students to have success, all the other students will also be able to be successful, and you will inevitably build a truly inclusive environment. Imagine how powerful this would be if the entire school got on board with this process. Go on, take a risk, and be a trendsetter!

- **Ditch the weekly spelling and grammar tests**. Instead, engage in meaningful conversations. It's a myth that ELLs need to memorize a weekly list of vocabulary in order to master academic language. The practice of science, for instance, has very little to do with defining key words; it has to do with doing, observing, forming thoughts, recording, and sharing those thoughts and opinions to build knowledge and expand prior knowledge. Key terminology needs to have contextual meaning attached to it, along with practical application, for true understanding to occur.

- **Dream Big.** Encourage all students to think big, and don't crush their dreams! Although these dreams may seem far-fetched now, for the sake of creativity and opportunity they are crucial. Remember if we encourage students to take risks and fail without fear, they can decide for themselves what will become realistic and what will not.

- **Use "No" to Fuel the Fire.** Luckily, from a young age I was taught to overcome adversity by using negative thoughts or comments made towards me to fuel my motivation and drive. My parents and sports coaches taught me to channel adversity into opportunity for growth rather than negative thinking. One junior hockey coach cut me from his team in my rookie year, telling me I would never play a game in the league. Not only did this motivate me to sign a contract with a team in a neighbouring city, it fuelled me to work hard and finish in the top three rookies in the league for most improved player. Help children use challenge and adversity to fuel their inner flame.

- **Take the High Road.** Just because you tried something and it was an epic fail doesn't mean you can never try it again. Just because you got fired from the donut store doesn't mean you can never work in the food industry again. Encourage kids to learn to take another route, angle, or pathway to reach their desired destination.

- **What's on the Inside Counts.** Help students realize that the adage about beauty being skin deep only refers to physical beauty. Teach them that there are many different types of internal beauty. Don't let negative self-perceptions about language barriers or image prevent them from putting themselves out there. Encourage them to join clubs, to socialize with a broad range of students, and to surround themselves with people who will help them grow.

- **Practice Positive Self-talk.** Phyllis L. Fagell, a school counselor who wrote, "10 Ways to Help Kids Take Risks in a World of 'No's," says people have more than 20,000 thoughts a day and 80% of them are negative (Fagell, 2016, para. 15). Our brains are hard-wired to pay more attention to bad experiences than to good ones. That can take a toll. You assume that you wouldn't lie to yourself, but you do. You and your students may be overly self-critical or exaggerate problems. Monitor your thoughts so they don't hinder you, and help your students do the same.

- **Be the Biggest Cheerleader.** Be your students' biggest advocate. Let them know you *have their back* in difficult situations, and that you will help them through it, without doing it for them. You know how good it feels to be supported in a challenge, like running a marathon. If you constantly had someone screaming at you from the sidelines that you won't succeed, you would have a much more difficult time. This same concept applied to language acquisition would leave us in a world of monolingual, non-risk taking strangers! Cheer loudly and proudly — after all, you are mentoring our future leaders!

- **Everyone has a story.** Take the time to listen.

Ideas to try with colleagues or in the classroom

Think about how you will better support your ELLs moving forward. What learning do you need to do? What is your next step in helping students fail productively?

Place a picture of one of your ELLs in the middle of a page. Now intentionally plan your lesson around this student by using these four subheadings in each corner of the page:
1. What prior knowledge do they need?
2. What scaffolding do I need to do?
3. What do I expect them to produce?
4. How will I assess or measure growth?

Chapter 4

Failure Through the Years

Remember your dreams and fight for them. You must know what you want from life. There is just one thing that makes your dream become impossible: the fear of failure.

—Paulo Coelho

In the last chapter, we touched on the perceptions that students of different ages have of failure based on a wide cross-section of different cultural backgrounds. This informal study was limited in scope and neither accounted for native English learners nor educators. In this chapter, we will look at how the idea of failure evolves through life, both for students and for educators. One belief is that in the early years of education, if educators can figure out what conditions and environments contribute to positive interactions between children and school, then an early trajectory can set them on a positive pathway towards future success (Hamre & Pianta, 2005; Hamre, Pianta, Downer, & Mashburn, 2005).

Positive relationships with teachers, in particular, predict gains in student engagement as students move from early years, to middle school, through high school. These teacher–student relationships increase motivation to learn, producing greater academic achievement (Pianta, Hamre, & Allen, 2012, p. 366). One aspect is that the relationship between teacher and student influences engagement and therefore success. The assumption is that students who are more engaged in school will become more engaged in their own futures. This line of thinking implies that students become increasingly aware of their interests and academic capabilities as they journey from elementary school through higher education. Once they gain that self-knowledge, it allows them to align, or realign their educational plans, which may mean changing their career goals, for example.

I can speak to this from experience. I had dreams of being a professional athlete. I even spoke with several scouts, but ended up not being drafted by either the National Hockey League (NHL) or Major League Baseball (MLB). I then realized my slim chances of ever playing professional sports. Based on the relationships I had with educators in secondary school, I realized I was passionate about sports therapy and that a career in that field would be a natural fit. I then realized the academic requirements and the competitive nature of being accepted into one of these programs. These same educators, several sports coaches, and my parents pointed out that I was good at dealing with people and showed some leadership qualities. This pushed me towards a degree in psychology. Once again my relationship with educators — and a supervisor at one of my student-work placements — shifted my thinking towards education rather than becoming a psychologist. These relationships helped bring out the best in me, which in turn helped me to be more successful and more realistic about my career path.

In fact, researchers have analyzed student ambitions and aspirations and to what extent they are unrealistic or unachievable, perhaps setting themselves up for failure (Reynolds, Stewart, Macdonald, & Sischo, 2006, p. 187). Other research has looked at the possibility that college/university students have unclear or undeveloped plans (Romano & Palmer, 2015, p. 74), or that they are involved in academic and career "experiments" and are therefore less committed to finishing and graduating than those who have a clear plan (Romano & Palmer, 2015, p. 115). There is also a notion that some student aspirations are unrealistic; perhaps they themselves aren't convinced that they are attainable either (Adelman, 2005).

Perhaps we need to pay greater attention to students with unclear or underdeveloped plans as they progress through school. Regardless of age or level within the school system, Mohan Kumar (2014) suggests that we encourage eight specific strategies to promote student potential toward building resilience and overcoming failure in a positive way:

1. **Connectedness**: Resilient people rely on a whole network of others to help them through tough situations and in turn reciprocate this support to help others when they need help. It's just as important to accept help as to give it (Kumar, 2014, para. 16).

2. **Acceptance**: Resilient people accept change. They see change as an opportunity for growth rather than an obstacle in their way (Kumar, 2014, para. 17).

3. **Communication**: Resilient people are always working on improving their communication skills. They are able to verbalize their challenges and need for support. They communicate the strategies they've tried and ask for help devising new ones. They are also active listeners and see suggestions from others as a sign of strength (Kumar, 2014, para. 18).

4. **Curiosity**: Resilient people exercise a sense of wonder. They are curious about what got them into the situation and how they will pull through it. They are curious about the outcome and about how the potential worst-case scenario might play out. They are reflective and aware of how their behaviour will affect those around them (Kumar, 2014, para. 19).

5. **Crisis Management**: Resilient people learn that keeping a cool head during times of stress helps them to remain optimistic. They quickly overcome the feeling of loss of control and move into action by making educated and decisive decisions. They do not bury their heads in the sand in hopes that the issue will disappear (Kumar, 2014, para. 20).

6. **Confidence**: Resilient people see themselves as positive influencers. They work hard to maintain a positive self-image and promote a strong and inclusive environment around them. They are decisive and confident in the face of adversity (Kumar, 2014, para. 21).

7. **Focus**: Resilient people make short-term goals and stay laser focused on achieving them. They break down situations into manageable tasks that can be tackled. They are realistic,

reasonable, and ambitious. They keep the long-term goal in mind as they hit the short-term targets and build success based on the small gains (Kumar, 2014, para. 22).

8. **Creativity**: Resilient people demonstrate and promote creativity. Learning new artistic techniques in cooking, dance, art, or music helps increase resilience. The positivity of artistic expression is infectious, allowing people to grow and heal (Kumar, 2014, para. 23).

Kumar's CR8 Model of Resilience

© Mohan Kumar 2014

Think of the possibilities! If we made the changes that Kumar suggests, students would revise and refine their learning experiences in a much richer, fuller manner. In addition, teachers would model failure as part of their professional growth and students, from a very young age, would see themselves as co-learners, as both receivers *and* givers of knowledge.

Another concern is that failure can lead to a loss of enthusiasm, and so too can the opposite prove true — loss of enthusiasm due to other factors can lead to failure. In his book *Stratosphere*, Michael Fullan looked at loss of enthusiasm for school from Kindergarten through Grade 12, finding that children begin school with almost boundless enthusiasm and then lose interest, which reaches a low point in Grade 9 when only a third of students are still enthusiastic. By Grade 12, enthusiasm makes a bit of a comeback with almost half of students engaged. But that still leaves 55% of Grade 12 students *un*enthusiastic. And how might that impact their career path?

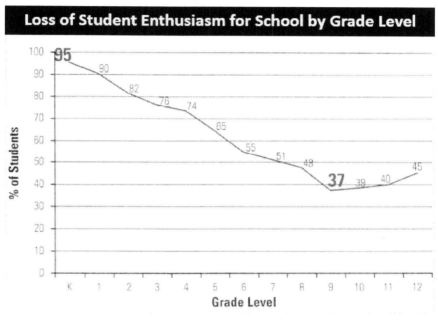

Loss of Student Enthusiasm for School by Grade Level

From Stratosphere (2013) by Michael Fullan (p.29)

This loss of enthusiasm could be caused by the increased demands of the curriculum and the associated increased expectations, the new environment of a bigger school, or even the over-scheduling of teenagers' lives. Clearly, many factors can lead to a lack of enthusiasm as students progress through high school. I wonder what this graph might look like, however, if we promoted Peter Senge's definition of failure — "a shortfall, evidence of the gap between vision and current reality. Failure is an opportunity for learning about inaccurate pictures of current reality, about strategies that didn't work as expected, about the clarity of a vision" (Senge, 2006, p. 143). Regardless of the reasons for this loss of enthusiasm, it's interesting to note the way it could correlate to failure, which is something we should stay curious about as educators.

In his article "Why Kids Need to Fail to Succeed in School," Gordon M. Grant interviewed Paul Tough, author of *How Children Succeed: Grit, Curiosity, and the Hidden Power of Character*. Tough discusses the real differences between developing self-esteem and developing character, suggesting that we are confused about the two. He agrees that we could promote high self-esteem simply by praising everything students do, not challenging them in any way, removing all barriers, and making every excuse possible when they fail. On the other hand, if we want to develop character, we should do the exact opposite and let them fail. If we put them into situations where there is no clear-cut answer, they will need to exercise their own problem solving skills. This doesn't make them feel horrible about themselves, but rather encourages coping. We can acknowledge any failures along the way, discuss the situation, coach them through it, and offer tools and strategies for the future (Grant, 2012). If educators and parents devoted more time and effort towards building children's characters rather than their self-esteem, we would better prepare them to be more enthusiastic and engaged students as they progress through any education system.

If building character involves letting our children fail, learn from it, and continue to fail their way toward success (Grant, 2012), why are we not doing a good enough job of this? One issue is "helicopter parents," a term first introduced in Dr. Haim Ginott's 1971 book *Between Parent and Teenager* by teens who said their parents would hover over them like helicopters. Helicopter parenting means watching every move children make so they don't make mistakes. Parents "typically take too much responsibility for their children's experiences and, specifically, their successes or failures" according to Carolyn Daitch (Bayless, n.d., para. 2). This means everything from carrying a small child's backpack and completing homework assignments to selecting their high school and post-secondary courses, and even attempting to sit in on job interviews. This parenting style stifles independence completely, preventing children from experiencing failure.

Did this behaviour come out of the parents' own fear of failure? Brooke Donatone thinks so. She believes that the big problem is not that students think too highly *of* themselves, but that they are unable to think *for* themselves, especially in situations of conflict negotiation (Donatone, 2013, para. 8). The issue with helicopter parenting is that it doesn't allow children to wrestle with conflict and disappointment by themselves so they can develop a little more resilience with each tough situation. Although we can't compensate for bad parenting, it is still our responsibility as educators to challenge this. We need to communicate openly and often with parents to promote the idea that they would be doing their children a service by taking a step back and allowing them to flourish. If this seems counterintuitive to a parent, we must support them in supporting their children along the way. It's better to coach them through failure than to ignore or shy away from it, leaving them ill prepared to deal with failure later in life.

This became very clear early in my teaching career with a dedicated student struggling to do well in math. This student understood the concepts and could apply then on a daily basis in class; however, he struggled when asked to write a test. When I met with his parents to explain the discrepancies in his daily understanding versus performance, they wanted to intervene. They asked to attend classes, to sit with him while he wrote tests, to reduce his sports time, and to increase his homework. As we continued the conversation, *their* career plan for his future also became clear. His mom wanted him to attend a specific university, graduate with a specific doctoral degree, make a specific amount of money, and be "successful." The following day, the counter-productiveness of his parents' approach was abundantly clear. When I spoke with him, he explained that he simply gets anxious on tests for fear of not doing well and having his parents think he's a failure.

As an administrator, I see helicopter parenting on a regular basis, beginning as early as Kindergarten. I've seen parents insist on carrying their child's backpack to school, walk them to class, then literally hover at the door — seemingly waiting for that first tear to drip so they can swoop in and rescue them from the hardship. I've also seen that when a student experiences an assessment result — especially a first one — that doesn't meet parental expectations, it can be followed by an immediate request to switch teachers or classrooms. In terms of classroom misbehaviour, I frequently get parental push back. Their child would never do that, or it's because they didn't get enough sleep, or because the teacher gives too much homework. This doesn't help their child learn and grow; in fact, allowing students to struggle is exactly what they need. If students can work through these situations when the stakes are low, it helps them learn how not to avoid, flee, or shut down in future when the stakes will likely be much higher. Coaching parents through the process of allowing their children to experience failure without fear allows them to see children as capable of developing resilience in the face of failure, even if the level of achievement may not be exactly what the parents "dreamt it would be."

Ideas to try with colleagues or in the classroom

Reflect on your own failures through your career. Are you getting better at learning from them or are you taking them more personally?

Use Kumar's Venn diagram to brainstorm with students, colleagues, or yourself what significance the overlapping circles would have in developing greater resilience.

What new strategies can you use to communicate with parents so that they are included and involved in their child's education without being overbearing and negatively influencing the child's experience?

Chapter 5

Overcoming the Fear of Failure

If I'm being rejected from one thing, it's really just the path
redirecting me elsewhere to where I'm supposed to be.
—Amani Al-Khatahtbeh, Founder of MuslimGirl

I n this chapter, we will explore how stress negatively affects learning
outcomes, how marks and grades aren't always the predictors of future success, and how drive and motivation are crucial to overcome the
fear of failure — for both students and educators. After all, society has
evolved in the direction of new and potentially multiple different career
pathways. This uncertainty can lead to stress, and we need to learn to
channel that toward success. It is daunting for us to keep up with these
changes, let alone try to prepare students for these moving targets, but
it begins with us. Once the education system embraces the idea that education should be more than marks and grades, it could open the door
to innovation and a new type of student.

School can be a turbulent place, not always designed to support
students who struggle with the current methods or system. We must
change the narrative to better support all our students for a workforce
that does not yet exist. Science, technology, engineering, and math
(STEM) skills are becoming more necessary to succeed in the professional world. With the introduction of artificial intelligence (AI), the
need for such skills will increase dramatically over the coming decade.
A report by PricewaterhouseCoopers (PwC) anticipates that 40% of US
jobs will be replaced by robots and AI by the early 2030s. Financial
services face an even higher risk of turnover with 61% of jobs being

replaced by machines (Lovell, 2017). It is clear that schools need to find engaging ways to involve students, perhaps especially those who don't fit the mold of a traditional A+ student. Let's look at one parent's example of a situation we want to avoid.

When School Doesn't Work

Writing about her son's experiences with school, Anna Keller highlights the fact that school can't simply be a cookie-cutter model applied to all children. Her blog "What we did when our son was failing school" describes a boy who was very bright, naturally gifted in the arts, and a wonderful, non-confrontational brother, yet a horrible student. The impact on her family was frustrating and draining. Frequent tears, broken pencils, torn and crumpled up assignments, yelling, and door slamming were regular occurrences at home. His teachers said he was very capable but unwilling to put in the effort and not able to pay attention class. They hoped that the lightbulb would eventually turn on for him. Keller felt as if the school was judging her ability to parent, thinking that if she would only discipline him and hold him more accountable that suddenly he would turn it around. She tried giving praise, being proactive, using positive reward systems, and schedules, yet he just didn't respond to any of them. Her son had great intentions and desperately wanted the glowing results of achieving good grades but he simply didn't have the stamina, so study plans repeatedly fell apart, leaving him feeling deflated. Despite good relationships with friends and teachers, he was miserable, which dragged the entire family down with him (Keller, 2013).

Currently, education systems aren't always structurally and systematically set up to embrace and nurture the range and diversity of students. It is our responsibility as educators to fight for a more universally accommodating system. By planning lessons and units with our most at-risk children at the forefront, we are more likely to avoid situations where they disengage with school. By consulting with children and including their student voice, we shift our approach to be more inclusive of those the system is intended for. If we allow children to engage in their own natural curiosity, providing open-ended tasks that naturally promote the inquiry cycle, then children can take their learning in different directions and feed off their interests. If we provide students with tasks for which we don't know the outcome — that don't have a prescriptive right or wrong answer — it directly models our acceptance of failure as part of the learning process. Displaying our own vulnerability in this way would help create a safe learning environment that promotes risk taking and diminishes the feeling and fear of failure.

Stress in Students

According to the American Psychological Association's Christopher Munsey, what children say is stressing them versus what parents believe is causing them stress are two different things. He believes this discrepancy could have long-term effects on the mental health of children if we don't take the time to listen and take that information at face value (Munsey, 2010, p. 22).

Medical doctor Stephen Dowshen, in his article "Childhood Stress," states that stress occurs when we feel like we can't respond to the needs and demands that society puts on us, or those we put on ourselves. These demands can come from either external or internal sources and it's how we respond to them that can create stress. External sources include family, jobs, friends, school, interviews, parenting, and financial decisions. Stress often stems from what *we think we should be doing* versus what *we're actually able to do*. Even kids feel this same push and pull in their day-to-day flow, so as adults we need to be aware of this and support children when they are feeling overwhelmed or anxious. For example, right from preschool to college, separation from parents when attending school can cause children stress. As the stakes get higher, academic, social, and emotional pressures too can create stress (Dowshen, 2015).

Children aged 8 to 17 report that what stresses them the most include family finances, doing well in school, and getting into good colleges (Munsey, 2010, p. 22). It amazes me that children as young as eight are concerned about their family's financial situation. How much baggage are children carrying with them every day as they come through our school's front doors? Because of these stressors, they also report headaches, sleeplessness, and upset stomachs. The most concerning part is that these symptoms of stress may go undetected and may not be dealt with in the appropriate manner (Munsey, 2010, p. 22).

In Munsey's publication "The Kids Aren't All Right," he references Katherine Nordal, the American Psychological Association's executive director for professional practice, noting that parents and teachers need to listen, creating safe and open environments where children feel comfortable coming forward with their concerns. This is critical because, if untreated, ongoing stress leads to chronic stress, which can cause both physical and psychological complications (Munsey, 2010, p. 22). To help parents reduce stress for their children, Amy Przeworski (2013) suggests twelve tips:

1. **Encourage children to face their fears:** When children learn to face their fears — rather than run away or be rescued from them — they naturally learn that stress is a short-term response that they can manage on their own. They realize that they are mentally strong and that by facing their fears, they empower themselves creating a healthy mind and body (para. 2).

2. **It's okay to be imperfect:** All too often, we focus on outcomes to determine success in school, sports, and life in general. If we value a certain grade as the benchmark for success in school, then we allow marks to determine success. It's much better if we can value the process, let kids make mistakes, and praise them for overcoming them rather than praising the grade (para. 3).

3. **Focus on the positives:** It's very easy for kids to get caught up comparing themselves negatively to others, especially on social media. Focus on your child's positive qualities and catch them doing positive things. Simple recognition from an adult motivates them to continue to think positive thoughts and model positive behaviour (para. 4).

4. **Promote fun and enjoyment:** In our busy, overscheduled world, we need to plan time for kids just to relax and have

fun. We may think that sports and competitive activities are what children need, but they can also be stressful. Plan some time each week to do fun activities with your children: playing a board game, watching a movie, playing cards, doing yoga, riding a bike, or blowing bubbles. Whatever it is that they enjoy, plan to do it often (para. 5).

5. **Model self-care:** If you expect your children to take good care of themselves, then you need to start by modelling it yourself. This includes everything from eating healthy, exercising, smiling, and treating others with respect. Remember, kindness is contagious. When you are in stressful situation, acknowledge it and model how you too are facing your fears and using coping strategies (para. 6).

6. **Reward brave behaviour:** Recognize and predict tough situations for your child when you know they will need to deal with something difficult. Talk to them about it and help strategize. When they demonstrate bravery, reward them with positive words, physical rewards like hugs and high fives, and even tangible rewards like small treats (para. 7).

7. **Encourage good sleep hygiene:** When life becomes unpredictable, it becomes stressful, so routines are crucial for you to model with your child. Avoid unpredictability by setting a non-negotiable bedtime. Good sleep hygiene helps with memory, behaviour, attitude, and physical growth. Reserve the last half hour before bedtime for something calming like reading a story or listening to quiet music (para. 8).

8. **Encourage conversations:** Encourage your child to talk about their stress and anxiety as part of everyday conversations. This allows them to get stressful situations off their chest and deal with them in proactive ways. Demonstrate that you are listening and not just shrugging it off. Say things like, "I see that you are feeling anxious about this, how can I help?" Offer assistance and reassure them that they can overcome the stressful situation, first together and then on their own (para. 9).

9. **Help them problem solve:** Now that you have modelled to your child that you are an active listener and can offer help, you need to follow through. Take a co-problem solver approach where you are asking questions like, "Tell me more about...," "I wonder where you might start to work through this," or "What would it look like if this was solved perfectly?" This approach does not let them off the hook for doing the thinking. Remember, you are coaching them to be independent problem solvers (para. 10).

10. **Stay calm:** Children perceive your emotions. If they sense you are stressed or panicked about something, they will be too. This starts in infancy when a baby falls down, cries, and looks to the parent for a response. If the response is to gasp aloud, then we reinforce the stress and panic. Your kids need to see you as a calming influence and they too will have a better chance of modelling this same behaviour. Keep calm, and fail on (para. 11).

11. **Promote relaxation:** Never underestimate the power of relaxation. Basic relaxation strategies are a necessity to navigate this busy world. Remind your child to use breathing exercise like taking 3–5 deep breaths — in through the nose and out through the mouth — when they are feeling overwhelmed. Another strategy is to imagine that they are blowing up an imaginary balloon. Other strategies like having them imagine a relaxing location like the beach or swinging in the park can also help (para. 12).

12. **Never give up:** Recognize that stress can change over time so what might have worked in the past may not still be working. As children grow older, their needs change so try new stress reduction strategies to keep adapting (Przeworski, 2013, para. 13).

The Canadian Organization of University and College Health (2007) found that post-secondary students are no strangers to stress. More than 30,000 students were surveyed and the results were alarming.

Not only did students report feeling stressed, 90% reported feeling overwhelmed by their academic workload, 50% felt hopeless, and 63% felt very lonely (Miller, 2013, para. 4). The study's findings on the issue of suicide were both horrifying and eye opening: 9.5% of students indicated that they had seriously considered taking their own lives in the past year, while 1.3% said they had attempted suicide (Miller, 2013, para. 9).

Stress levels aren't restricted to college, university, and secondary school students; kids much younger also have stress. Daniel Keating's 2017 *Psychology Today* article, "Dealing with Stress at School in an Age of Anxiety," states that children who experience adversity in their early years and have an ongoing high level of stress will have long-term implications later in life. This starts in the womb. Babies exposed to toxic stress have brains that are wired differently, including how their genes evolve. "Stress dysregulation" (SDR) is a common consequence of early adversity typically exhibited in students with a clinical mental health diagnosis, affecting how students demonstrate their behaviour at home and in the classroom. These behaviours can be violent, aggressive, and difficult for the child to regulate, affecting not only the child themselves but other children around them (Keating, 2017, para. 3). Research findings also show that stress is contagious at a physiological level (Palumbo et al., 2017), making for a challenging learning environment for students, educators, and educational leaders (Keating, 2017, para. 5).

An online survey, conducted by Harris Interactive on behalf of the Practice Directorate's ongoing Mind/Body Health public education campaign, polled a nationally representative sample of 1,568 adults in July and August of 2010. Additional results were obtained for children ages 8 to 17 from a YouthQuery survey of 1,206 young people, also conducted online by Harris Interactive in August (Munsey, 2010). This research reinforces the importance of our schools being safe and inclusive places for students — not merely somewhere to attend. According to Rowe (2014), we can generally see three types of stress responses in children:

- **Positive stress response** is healthy and promotes growth and development. Situations like meeting new friends, walking late in to a room full of people, switching schools, or starting to play sports on a new team are examples. These situations provide opportunities for real life practice at developing positive responses to common events (Rowe, 2014, para. 2).

- **Manageable stress response** occurs when your body alerts you to larger stresses than everyday occurrences. Unhealthy relationships, parent divorce, or serious illnesses are examples. These situations are hard to deal with but children who have pulled through them would describe them as tolerable over time (Rowe, 2014, para. 6).

- **Toxic stress response** happens when children are exposed to serious levels of ongoing stress or even multiple different stressors at the same time. Exposure to violence, neglect, and social, emotional, or physical abuse are examples. This level of stress is layered with children not getting the proper adult supports required to deal with the stress. The long-term effects, both in terms of physical and mental development, can contribute to a lack of trust in new relationships (Rowe, 2014, para. 16).

If we begin to teach the idea of failure without fear — right from the beginning in the first year of school — we can promote the concept of positive stress by being supportive adults when students struggle to take risks. This will create positive learning environments that support students as they move through the challenges life throws at them and help them shape their future. If we do this, we will better prepare students to cope with more adverse stressors.

The amount of anxiety and stress I see starting in kindergarten classrooms — especially as we move through standardized testing — reinforces the idea of creating safe environments where children are respected. We have a moral responsibility — beginning in kindergarten — to prepare students to be flexible thinkers and to develop the ability to learn from negative experiences as part of their personal growth. Most stress that students experience is due to the fear of failure — not wanting to disappoint parents and teachers or the fear of outperforming or being outperformed by their peers.

Nobody likes to fail; in fact, the fear of failure can have a direct impact on how children learn. A study of 1,000 students conducted by the *British Journal of Educational Psychology* found that students who had a fear of failing adopted learning as a way to stroke their egos. They learned simply to improve their social status, however, not because they were interested in learning or improving themselves. The study also found that these students were less likely to acquire new learning skills and were more likely to cheat to get by (Michou, Vansteenkiste, Mouratidis, & Lens 2014, para. 3). Beyond stress having an effect on how students learn, it can affect the decisions students make about their learning needs. A system that focuses on results as the hallmarks of achievement must acknowledge how stressful that approach can be. Marks and grades cannot be the sole indicators of success or we truly are failing our children. We must reinforce the message that fearing failure isn't the answer. In fact, making mistakes helps demonstrate true learning — and that is absolutely the right answer!

My own experience with overcoming fear of failure was most prevalent during my Grade 11 year, when I had to work particularly hard in math. This was the year that marks and grades started to matter to me, since I was seeking scholarship opportunities to American colleges and universities. At this point, I truly had a fear of failure — and it caused me a great deal of anxiety and stress. I remember being fully aware that I needed to get extra math support if I wanted to achieve the levels necessary to meet the admission standards of certain American schools. But I was so afraid of making mistakes that I couldn't bring myself to show up for the help I required. One day when I was having a friendly conversation with a math teacher about my weekend sports activities, the notion of overcoming this fear seemed somewhat reasonable. In our conversation, he referred to how I must not be afraid of being on the big stage if I could perform with all those scouts watching despite the awareness of potentially "messing up." That was my "aha" moment. If I could manage anxiety in a large-group setting then surely I could do it one-on-one, or in a small group, working on math problems. The following day I approached him and asked if I could get extra help — a monumental step forward for me. The answer, of course, was yes, and that simple response changed my view of mathematics forever! Right away during our extra-help sessions, he realized that my fear of humiliation was preventing me from even *trying* to solve math problems. Over the next month, he coached me to overcome my fear of failure. I vividly remember the tipping point; he said, "Honestly — just try. Make a mistake. What's the worst that could happen… you will learn where you went wrong and then get it right?" That advice still resonates with me today. He had no idea what an impactful, moving experience that was for me. Well, now he does; one day we bumped into one another at a park with our families and I told him. It was the starting point for overcoming my fear of failure.

Grades Don't Predict Success

In August 2007, Sarah Scott published an article in *Maclean's Magazine* called "Do Grades Really Matter? A growing body of evidence suggests grades don't predict success — C+ students are the ones who end up running the world." As an example of how high school grades have no real long-term impact, Scott wrote about two students from Thornhill Secondary School in the early 1970s. Mike and Mark Cowie were identical twins who didn't pay much attention to their schoolwork. They were more interested in other things, like working at a garage after school to pay for their cars. They were bored in the classroom and didn't see any practical use for the curriculum.

The Cowie brothers went on to become two of Canada's most successful commercial real-estate brokers, learning more from their interactions with people outside of school than from books. Reading people's body language, how they sit, and how they say things is what made them so successful. It was easy for them to tune out high school English class because their interest levels were low and there wasn't anything for them to do with their hands. Tuning out got them C to C+ grades with comments on their report cards about needing to put in more effort. In their case (and in mine), these bored students didn't fit the mold of school and didn't exhibit the "typical" student outcomes. In my case, I was polite, respectful, and did what I was asked. I wasn't rude or defiant with any of my teachers, but I was a C+ student... and I was just fine with that. For me, it was the perfect balance of what I saw as input versus output. For the amount of input I was giving, in my opinion, I was receiving pretty good output. When I compared the amount of schoolwork (input) my friends did to get a B+ or A (output), it didn't seem worth it to me. That would have meant dedicating less time to practicing sports, being outside playing, and being with my friends. C+ seemed to be the sweet spot for me. I would have been frustrating to teach — as a teacher, I would have hated to teach me — because I was capable of achieving higher marks, but the payoff wasn't worth the investment for me. The Cowie brothers and I show how school grades aren't always predictors of success in life. So if we know these marks aren't true indicators of success, why don't we try new approaches, embrace failure, and connect with children in ways that motivate them to be the best person they can be?

Michael Thompson is a consultant, psychologist, and co-author (with Dan Kindlon) of the *New York Times* bestselling book, *Raising Cain: Protecting the Emotional Life of Boys* (1999). He also authored *Speaking of Boys: Answers to the Most-Asked Questions about Raising Sons* (2000). Thompson works with a variety of parents in North America who are anxious about their children's academic performance. He talks to them about how C grades are no indication that their children are doomed to never finding a successful career pathway. The letter grade is not a measure of their long-term capabilities, he says; rather it documents whether a teacher decided if their child understood the curriculum to their liking at a particular point in time. He says boys in particular find school boring and inefficient and are more interested in when it will be over so they can get back to their lives. They aren't as interested as girls are in proving to the teacher that they have understood the concept. Girls are more likely to want to impress their teachers with their academic performance and support each other in achieving better academic grades (Scott, 2007, para. 6).

Drive and Motivation

Presently, grades seem to be the most important driving force in education. I suggest that the focus should be on drive and motivation instead. As we just learned, grades are not necessarily a predictor of future success, even though they remain the barometer used to determine success and failure. If, instead of grades, we used drive and motivation as benchmarks, we would have students more likely to accept — even embrace — failure as part of the learning journey. Our goal should be to produce driven, motivated people. This is supported by what psychologists have learned about motivation, or drive. Harvard psychologist David McClelland proposed the Needs Theory (also known as the Three Needs Theory) in the 1960s, a model intended to explain how people's motivational needs are driven by achievement, power, and affiliation. People driven by *achievement* like to work alone; they like environments where their individual results can be easily measured. They don't like tasks that are seen as either too easy, as they see this as a waste of time, or too high risk, as they see luck playing a huge factor in the successful outcome rather than hard work and dedication (McClelland, n.d., para. 2). When *power* is a motivator, these people thrive in environments with strict discipline and high levels of completion. If there is a winner and a loser, these conditions are optimal for people driven by power. Group dynamics become difficult to manage as they thrive on individual status recognition (McClelland, n.d., para. 4). Lastly, the Needs Theory suggests that people are motivated by *affiliation*. These people thrive in social situations and work where the status of the group is more important than that of the individual. This gives them a sense of belonging and a feeling of being loved and wanted (McClelland, n.d., para. 3). Wouldn't it be powerful if organizations could hire staff members using these same principles? Rather than hire people based on marks and IQ scores, we should be considering what people have to offer outside of marks and grades. For instance, how do CEOs and principals handle difficult decisions, how do they de-escalate frustrated stakeholders, and how do they promote success in a positive and supportive way? In education, there is certainly a shift towards designing interviews to allow candidates to demonstrate these skills. Often school visits and job shadowing allow boards and districts to hire candidates with high social-emotional intelligence. Instead of just relying on marks and IQ, employers should identify the behaviours that distinguish people who succeed in that type of position. If we hire and assign people to positions where the behaviour profile isn't a good fit with the environment, then we are actively setting them up to fail. By accounting for a multitude of factors besides grades, organizations are better equipped to pair personality types to the needs of the people they are serving. If they take a one-dimensional approach, their organization will reflect that (McClelland, n.d., para. 1).

Sara Scott's *Maclean's* article "Do Grades Really Matter?" offers support for moving away from a grades-based focus. Scott's article argues that drive is crucial to becoming successful. Without drive, we lack the true passion necessary to achieve success. Scott describes a study done by Rena Subotnik, who looked at 210 graduates of Hunter College Elementary School in Manhattan, a school for intellectually gifted children who were not affected by poverty. These students had a mean IQ score of 157, which is higher than over 99% of people. These students, by all accounts, were seen as affluent over-achievers who should do well in school and ultimately, be very successful in life. When these children were followed into adulthood, they were found to be good, contributing citizens, but not outstandingly successful. Why not? The theory is that they lacked drive, which prevented them from climbing to the top. Drive is a huge factor for students achieving their goals and rising above others trying to achieve similar goals (Scott, 2007, para. 12).

Drive took me from being a C student to a B+ student in a single school year. There were many reasons for this, but drive was certainly the biggest factor. I had been content with C's because the input/output balanced my academic life with my social and athletic endeavours. This worked until I saw the opportunity to earn a scholarship. My focus on my athletic goals meant that I started to catch the eye of baseball scouts, including American Division 1 schools for both baseball and track and field. Once scouts started calling and emailing me, I realized that this dream could become a reality. It wasn't until one of the track and field coaches from Harvard asked what my marks were that I realized I still had a lot of work to do to make this dream come true. Overnight, my drive for academic achievement shifted! Suddenly I was hungry for the academic success that would bring me athletic scholarships. Once I started getting offers from schools my math teacher allowed me to use these numbers as part of our algebra lessons to compare and evaluate what were my best offers. This contributed to my drive to thrive both academically and athletically. I changed my mindset and soon started putting more hours towards my studies. I asked questions of successful students around me to improve my approach to learning and studying. My thought process changed from contented to driven, wanting to separate myself from the pack. This hunger pushed me past a person on my track team who had been faster than I was and getting better marks than I was. I received seven scholarship offers in total (four for track and field and three for baseball).

What Can Teachers/Educators Do?

As educators, we need to adapt to help students prepare for the future. I know that sounds obvious, but sometimes we become so caught up in making sure we cover the curriculum that we forget the end goal. Schools, school boards, and provinces need to work more closely with the business world/industry to set students up for success in the labour force. They need to stay current with labour trends to enable educators to know what to focus on in order to create driven, motivated graduates. Once students have the knowledge of how to learn from failure, they develop confidence and leave school with a brighter future. My research into this subject led me to develop this list of nine strategies for educators as a suggested starting point to help address the rapidly changing job markets and career paths:

1. **Let students fail toward their passion:** Students often stumble upon their passions through trial and error. Starting in Kindergarten, expose students to different opportunities to find their passions. Ryan Porter, CEO and founder of Raise Your Flag, runs an online, career-path recruitment website where

he and his team map out potential career paths. They believe that if we can help connect young people to meaningful career paths, to work that has a purpose, the world will be a tangibly better place to live, work, and play. Some companies care more about hiring people with passion, drive, and motivation than they do about that piece of paper the system promotes. When young workers with purpose meet change-making companies, the companies thrive and young employees learn, progress, and give back to society.

2. **Promote flexible thinking and problem solving:** According to Susan Adams, in her 2013 *Forbes Magazine* article, these were the top ten most "looked for" employment attributes in our highly competitive world:

    1. Ability to work in a team
    2. Ability to make decisions and solve problems
    3. Ability to plan, organize, and prioritize work
    4. Ability to communicate verbally with people inside and outside an organization
    5. Ability to obtain and process information
    6. Ability to analyze quantitative data
    7. Technical knowledge related to the job
    8. Proficiency with computer software programs
    9. Ability to create and/or edit written reports
    10. Ability to sell to and influence others (Adams, 2013)

3. **Teach learning skills:** In Ontario, where I work, we must report on our students' learning skills three times a year. The categories for assessing, evaluating, and reporting on student achievement from Kindergarten to Grade 12 are outlined in Ontario's comprehensive policy, *Growing Success: Assessment, Evaluation and Reporting in Ontario's Schools*:

Learning Skills and Work Habits	Sample Behaviours
Responsibility	The student: ■ fulfills responsibilities and commitments within the learning environment; ■ completes and submits classwork, homework, and assignments according to agreed-upon timelines; and, ■ takes responsibility for and manages own behaviour.
Organization	The student: ■ devises and follows a plan and process for completing work and tasks; ■ establishes priorities and manages time to complete tasks and achieve goals; and, ■ identifies, gathers, evaluates, and uses information, technology, and resources to complete tasks.
Independent Work	The student: ■ independently monitors, assesses, and revises plans to complete tasks and meet goals; and, ■ uses class time appropriately to complete tasks.
Collaboration	The student: ■ accepts various roles and an equitable share of work in a group; ■ responds positively to the ideas, opinions, values, and traditions of others; ■ builds healthy peer-to-peer relationships through personal and media-assisted interactions; ■ works with others to resolve conflicts and build consensus to achieve group goals; and, ■ shares information, resources, and expertise, and promotes critical thinking to solve problems and make decisions.

Initiative	**The student:**
	■ looks for and acts on new ideas and opportunities for learning;
	■ demonstrates the capacity for innovation and a willingness to take risks;
	■ demonstrates curiosity and interest in learning;
	■ approaches new tasks with a positive attitude; and,
	■ recognizes and advocates appropriately for the rights of self and others.
Self-Regulation	The student:
	■ sets own individual goals and monitors progress towards achieving them;
	■ seeks clarification or assistance when needed;
	■ assesses and reflects critically on own strengths, needs, and interests;
	■ identifies learning opportunities, choices, and strategies to meet personal needs and achieve goals; and,
	■ perseveres and makes an effort when responding to challenges.

Source: Ontario Ministry of Education, 2010b.

Students neither know what the learning skills are for which they are being assessed nor know what the expectations or standards are in order to achieve "excellent" or "good" in each area. These are arbitrarily determined by teachers with very vague criteria being communicated to our students. Districts, school leaders, and teachers need to dedicate more time to collaborating on determining what would constitute an "excellent" standard in each of the areas for each grade. Perhaps there needs to be a new "Teacher will..." section in the right-hand column. This is our opportunity to teach exactly what industry is telling us our future employees need.

4. **Replace marks:** Replace marks with feedback to help encourage students. We want them to be motivated to improve their work as opposed to getting dejected and giving up *or* thinking that there is nothing left to learn. Are we forcing the fear of failure

upon kids ourselves? Perhaps we make them feel incompetent or inadequate by sticking a number, a letter grade, or a reading level on every piece of their work, right from a young age. Grades may be useful for educators to identify where a child is in their learning and their entry point for instruction, but must we share this information with children? Might we start to see more impactful learning — and subsequently more driven students helping make societal changes — if we provided only thoughtful commentary rather than marks?

5. **Incorporate websites like myblueprint.ca:** This site provides different levels to help students build a portfolio of strengths and areas of interests. It also incorporates gaming components to allow students to read and explore different jobs and careers. The Grade 8–12 platform is rich with information about employment sectors, jobs, how much money they would make, what education pathway to follow, and what institutions offer the courses needed. It also has a resume-writing component that can be shared directly with employers, and it allows students to compile a digital portfolio to present to prospective employers. Just think of the power of bringing this into your instructional repertoire as real and relevant learning that is differentiated based on interest and curiosity. Not only are students meeting the required curriculum expectations, they are being educated about society and the world around them.

6. **Build community connections:** Invite community partners into your school or go visit them. If this isn't possible, visit via technology. Sites like Virtual Researchers on Call[5] allow you to connect with "experts" in the field to help bring your curriculum to life. This provides opportunities for students to become inspired, empowered, and curious. Even better, it provides a safety net for failure.

7. **Emphasize digital inclusion:** Digitization is redefining both how we work *and* the jobs and types of work that exist. Daily

---

5   www.vroc.ca

activities, like accessing files in the cloud, making purchases online, or even a simple email attachment may be familiar tasks, but not everyone can claim these basic competencies. Some are still not online or equipped with the digital skills needed for their future jobs. Programs that promote digital inclusion are crucial for transition to the new economy (Lovell, 2017).

8. **Create psychological safety:** Google conducted a 2-year study demonstrating that "psychological safety" is a singular factor shared by successful teams (VanLeeuwen, 2017). Psychological safety refers to an environment where every voice around the table is heard and honoured, where risk taking is promoted and valued, where people feel safe to ask any questions, and where leaders and mangers let down their guard and admit vulnerability. The study found that it wasn't about assembling the "dream team" of the most highly qualified individuals, but rather those with drive and no fear of failure (VanLeeuwen, 2017). Noted futurist Rohit Talwar has famously said that students should expect hold 40 different jobs in ten completely different career paths in their lives and this is why it's so important to be flexible, resilient, and driven to achieve long-term goals (Harris, 2015). It is our responsibility to provide psychological safety for students, which allows them to develop the flexible mindset necessary to contribute positively to any team, in any sector, in any job, and not be afraid to fail.

Ideas to try with colleagues or in the classroom

Reflect on at least two ways you would have found to reduce school stress for the young person described at the beginning of the chapter in Anna Keller's blog, "What we did when our son was failing school."

What strategies will you implement to increase drive and motivation for all learners? How will you monitor your progress and the progress of students?

Change the landscape of learning by reducing the physical grades given, increasing your timely, meaningful, descriptive feedback, and then providing time for students to apply your suggestions. How can you teach students to improve their learning skills while reducing the number of grades that students see on their academic output? How can you create new criteria for success in your classroom?

Chapter 6

How Technology Integration, Gamification, and Game-Based Learning Support Failing Forward

Every maker of video games knows something that the makers of curriculum don't seem to understand. You'll never see a video game being advertised as being easy. Kids who do not like school will tell you it's not because it's too hard. It's because it's — boring.

—Seymour Papert

The world of gaming offers an environment in which failure, persistence, fun, and success exist symbiotically. Often, children *and* adults will persevere beyond what a non-game-playing person might believe simply to move forward to the next level. They see failure as opportunity, not as a reason to give up. Using the lessons of their failure to retry the same task from a different angle or approach in order to achieve their goal of passing the level is exactly the kind of thinking we should be instilling into school-based challenges. This chapter will examine how the gaming industry has prepared children to overcome failure, and how educators can embrace technology to help boost instruction and learning.

What can we learn from technology and gaming to reshape our education system in order to improve student outcomes? It would be easy to attribute this perseverance in reaching the next level simply to it being a fun activity; however, I don't believe it's that simple. Yes the games are fun, but beyond that they provide an intriguing and engaging outlet to express both curiosity and commitment, and games also provide natural opportunities to fail your way forward. In my experience, students like to be challenged and for the bar to be set high — two variables that make success even more gratifying. Game play is the same. Players don't generally begin with the mindset that they will breeze through each level effortlessly; they expect to fail and anticipate what they will do differently the next time. The most popular games aren't the easiest; they are the most interesting and challenging. We would serve our students well if we find a way to approach learning the same way.

In their *Journal of Educational Psychology* article "Unmotivated or Motivated to Fail," Krista De Castella, Don Byrne, and Martin Covington describe how all students want to be seen by others as smart and successful individuals capable of achieving their potential. If this potential is reached with very little effort, the perception is that they are naturally talented and are seen as smart. If, however, students make an effort but are not successful on the first attempt, they are seen as less smart and less capable of achieving success. This perception often leads people to avoid taking risks or putting forth a valiant effort for fear that failure will make them appear less capable. This, in turn, leads them to change their perception of what failure is and to make excuses for failure rather than accept the challenge of the journey or appreciate the process (De Castella, Byrne, & Covington, 2013, p. 861).

According to her *New York Times* bestselling book, *Reality is Broken*, author Jane McGonigal says that the more we fail, the more eager we are to do better. Failure feedback is a reward in itself. It makes us more engaged and more optimistic about our odds of success. Positive failure feedback reinforces our sense of control about our outcomes. When failure is associated with attempting to achieve a goal, people are more likely to remain optimistic and persevere rather than giving up. Without a goal, it's easy to quit. She goes on to explain that learning to stay urgently optimistic in the face of failure is an important emotional strength that we can learn in games and apply to our real lives (McGonigal, 2011, p. 67). Each time we fail while playing a game, we learn something new that adds to our curiosity and keeps us wanting more. It's when we have beaten the game — or even just mastered a level — that we become bored and start to seek out a new challenging adventure. A difficult game that demands that we think and fail repetitively in order to make progress towards reaching our goal is downright addictive!

Gaming versus Schooling

Much like gaming, schooling is hard and we need to help students mentally prepare themselves for learning and studying persistently. Students need to be pushed beyond their zone of proximal development. Only once we start to prepare students for this type of rigour, as well as model that as teachers we too can find learning tough, will we better mentally prepare students to become life-long learners. The tangible reward for this hard work is that the system gives students a diploma or degree that indicates they are prepared for the world ahead. Without the journey of learning through failure, however, it is entirely possible — if not likely — that the piece of paper does not represent preparedness. In order to do that properly, we need to interrupt the status quo — we need to create experiences that mimic society and create the understanding that life is hard. The gaming industry is already doing just that. In Kevin Dickinson's BigThink.com article, "Video Games and the Paradox of Failure," he explains how people actively seek out failure as a pastime. Although they are trying to avoid failure, they understand that it is necessary in order to move forward (Dickinson, 2018, para 8). The article also mentions that when people experience failure they learn even more about themselves. This is a concept that we should strive for in our classrooms, not only for children but also for the educators. Imagine a school system that created the conditions and environment where learning was challenging and engaging enough that children and adults sought out risk taking and embraced failure to learn even more. This idea of addressing lagging skills in a positive and productive manner in order to become a better-rounded person is what we should be striving for (Dickinson, 2018, para 9). Failure helps us to identify our weaknesses. With feedback and persistence, we can help each other overcome them by setting incremental goals to improve ourselves.

Dickinson also notes that players prefer games where they feel responsible for failure, not games where success is guaranteed. In a contest between a game in which the player has to make a decision to determine an outcome but will likely fail versus a game where simply clicking a button would determine the outcome for you, the former would win. In fact, many players handicap themselves, either by selecting a higher difficulty level or by creating self-imposed rules should a game's challenge grow too stale (Dickinson, 2018, para. 13). In education, we need to reinforce the idea that taking risks, and failing often and frequently, doesn't mean we are inadequate or incompetent. We just need to apply our new learning in different ways to expand our knowledge.

We can do this by designing our lessons to allow students to design, build/construct, fail, redesign, rebuild/reconstruct, fail, etc. One way of doing this is through project-based learning (PBL), which allows children to engage with a challenge or a question over time until it is solved. The *Buck Institute* for Education (BIE) is dedicated to improving 21st century teaching and learning through PBL. With PBL, teachers engage students in big ideas that force them to think beyond what they can research on the Internet in a matter of seconds. Often these projects take several days to several weeks to complete, promoting a cyclical process where students are introduced to authentic opportunities to make meaning to solve real-world problems. This process allows students to take risks, ask meaningful questions, uncover new ideas, make mistakes, learn from them, and continue learning (Buck Institute for Education, 2019, para. 4). We need to cycle through the design process continuously so that students can have authentic opportunities to challenge themselves, take risks, fail, learn from the failure, and reapply it in a way that constructs meaning. Constructing takes on two meanings: physically building something *and* constructing new thoughts, ideas, and visions that make the learning a part of our new schema.

What's Stopping Us?

Maybe *our own* fear of failure stops us from designing curriculum activities that provide opportunities for students to fail, and specifically to learn through the process of failing. This might also explain why we educators tend to shy away from technology-related activities. Perhaps we feel that we don't fully understand a process, a program, or a concept, and rather than model risk-taking and trying something new or uncomfortable, we choose a safer approach.

The effective use of technology is a perfect opportunity to promote failing forward. Assistive technology has opened doors, allowing some students to learn in individualized ways. By helping students explore the tools and discover what they are for and how they work, we naturally promote risk-taking through this use of technology. This helps students understand different types of software programs and online platforms so that they can choose what suits their learning needs and styles best. I once had a student who was afraid to start a writing task for fear of making a mistake, failing the assignment, and disappointing both teachers and parents. The assignment was broken down into chunks and was designed to build on each layer of success. The issue was purely the fear of what the written output would look like and sound like. The student had great ideas, but was reluctant to share them. I introduced this student to digital mind-mapping tools that would help organize ideas and thoughts while speaking them into a computer. The student learned that if they made mistakes in what they intended to say, the software still enabled them to collect their ideas and organize them into themes and paragraphs. The ability to manipulate the text digitally to reorganize the information was empowering. In fact, the student told me that this was the first time anyone had ever thought positively about them as a writer. I was overjoyed at how technology had helped this student overcome their fear of failure.

Of course, there is always a human element. If we are truly going to promote failure without fear, it is incumbent on educators to model digital responsibility and then trust the students. Throughout this process, we must teach them about the power of technology, about what is acceptable and what is not, and about how to leverage all of this information in a positive way. If we don't invest time here, we are setting them up for failure on many different levels. I don't mean a simple failure such as not knowing the best platform for doing a presentation; I mean not equipping them with the critical thinking skills necessary to navigate social media and the vastness of the evolving World Wide Web.

The Power of Technology

I remember the time I first showed a student with written-output difficulties how to use voice-to-text technology. She activated it, and started talking. It took her a minute to realize that her device was typing everything she said. Her eyes grew huge, she stood up, and starting jumping up and down shouting, "This is amazing; it's blowing my mind!"

Despite this mind-blowing opportunity to change a child's educational experience — and life in general — I have still heard educators who say "I don't do computers" or "That's cheating; they need to use pencil and paper" or "That's not fair!" That attitude would be equivalent to a doctor saying, "I don't do MRIs" or "It's cheating to use antibiotics." The time to fully integrate and utilize technology is now. "I don't do computers" would not be accepted in any other employment sector, so let's not accept it in education.

What Can Teachers/Educators Do?

The International Society for Technology in Education (ISTE, 2019a) is a non-profit advocacy organization that helps create more empowered learners worldwide. ISTE Standards provide clear guidelines for the skills and knowledge necessary to move forward in today's society. They provide a framework and a series of standards for students, educators, administrators, coaches, and computer science educators to rethink education and create innovative learning environments, to adapt to a constantly changing technological landscape, and to prepare students to enter an increasingly global economy (ISTE, 2019a, para. 1). In their standards for students, ISTE explains, "standards for teachers and students are designed to empower student voice and ensure that learning is a student-driven process" (ISTE, 2019c, para. 1). The standards are meant to help educators and system leaders worldwide to restructure schools and classrooms for digital-age learning (ISTE, 2019a).

Design Open Tasks With Choice

By designing open tasks and providing students with choices, we allow them the opportunity to exercise a growth mindset and approach tasks in the way best suited for them. When it comes to game-based learning, providing choice allows students to determine what types of games best suit their interests — and their entry point abilities — rather than have a one-size-fits-all approach. By introducing games as a way to learn, we also encourage trial and error methods of success. This allows students to attempt certain approaches to determine what's working, what's not working, and then make the necessary adjustments in their learning in order to have a more optimal outcome. The goal is to help students know *how* to learn, not just absorb exactly what you have taught them. Our learning goals need to be more about the process of learning rather than a checklist of tasks to complete. This idea is represented in ISTE standard 1a, "To set professional learning goals to explore and apply pedagogical approaches made possible by technology and reflect on their effectiveness" (ISTE, 2019b, para. 1).

Use Project-based Learning

As discussed earlier, project-based learning encourages students to answer complex questions through investigation. Having students collaborate, communicate, research, and present information allows them to think critically about issues that impact them and better prepares them to adapt to life's challenges as they grow and mature. Technological tools such as live streaming and social media provide ways for students to learn outside of the classroom by gathering information from experts in whatever field of interest is being studied. This use of technology allows for networking as well, which is a huge benefit if we think about the potential to connect virtually with people and organizations in ways that would not otherwise be possible. ISTE standard 5b — design authentic learning activities that align with content area standards and use digital tools and resources to maximize active, deep learning — supports this strategy nicely. ISTE standard 4c also supports this strategy by "encouraging us to use collaborative tools to expand students' authentic, real-world learning experiences by engaging virtually with experts, teams and students, locally and globally" (ISTE, 2019b, para. 4).

Model Problem Solving and Exploring

It is crucial that we model for students how we problem solve when we are stuck. Using self-talk and think-alouds allows students to hear your thought process as you problem solve your way through an obstacle. Modelling that they too will encounter struggles, which is a normal part of the learning process, not only validates students' experiences in facing challenges, it also empowers them to develop their drive to overcome barriers. Additionally, think-alouds can help students understand how you are navigating the use of a device or how you attempt to navigate the web. By doing this, you too will naturally discover new digital resources that you can share not only with students, but also with colleagues and parents. ISTE standard 2c suggests that we "model for colleagues the identification, exploration, evaluation, curation, and adoption of new digital resources and tools for learning" (ISTE, 2019b, para. 2).

Encourage Efficiencies

Technology allows students to access information in a variety of ways — for example audio files — that can make information more accessible. Such technology can help reduce the fear of failure because students can have information read to them by text-to-voice applications. Instantly, a student who can't read at grade level is now able to listen, change the voice recognition, change the pace, and even highlight the text as it reads the words. Students can also use voice-to-text software to capture their own words in written format, thus helping to eliminate barriers for students who struggle with written output. Another great technological helper for certain students would be mind-mapping applications. This type of software provides amazing opportunities for students to organize their thoughts in a variety of different ways (linear, horizontal, thought bubbles), helping students *see* the connections between their thoughts.

And what about the power of cloud-based learning? Imagine resources stored in a virtual environment, accessed from various web-enabled devices. Students can be in different physical spaces yet collaborating on the same working documents. With cloud-based drives, documents, and presentations, students can instantly update information, comment on each other's work, and provide and receive feedback. Not only does this promote efficiencies, it empowers the learner by allowing them to access, share, and receive information in new ways.

Connected to this idea are virtual classrooms that allow teachers to create lessons and assignments in a cloud-based environment. Students can turn in assignments online and be given personalized and timely feedback specific to the task and assignment. This feedback can be an audio file or text that could be read aloud to students. Students can access shared calendars so they know when assignments are upcoming and due. This is hugely powerful for students with multiple teachers and subjects. It allows students to better manage their time and help alleviate potential stress by more easily tracking whether they have multiple assignments due in the same week — or even on the same day. Educators must encourage the effective use of these tools and model for students how they make our lives easier. ISTE standard 7a speaks to this idea by suggesting that "we provide alternative ways for students to demonstrate competency and reflect on their learning using technology" (ISTE, 2019b, para. 7).

Provide a Variety of Ways to Present Knowledge

Whether you are implementing game-based learning, project-based learning, or an inquiry-based approach, the use of technology allows students to express their creativity and assert confidence in their learning. We must help students explore different technology tools to promote risk-taking and help them understand the various options for their work output. Using digital presentations, creating movies with applications, starting a blog, or vlog (video blog), are all ways that teachers can help students be less fearful of failing to produce quality work. These tools help to level the playing field, irrespective of learning styles, needs, or preferences. ISTE standard 2b encourages us to "advocate for equitable access to educational technology, digital content, and learning opportunities to meet the diverse needs of all students" (ISTE, 2019b, para. 2).

Flip your approach

Take a slightly different approach to your traditional classroom. Try providing students with shared lessons to watch at home the night before your class. This way they come to class prepared for what you are about to teach and you use your class time to coach students through difficult components of a task. This allows you to use technology to create, adapt, and personalize learning experiences that foster independent learning and accommodate learner differences and needs. It also makes it easier for students to feel prepared coming to class, eliminating potential anxiety. Creating material for students to refer back to while at home is also a great support for parents if they don't understand a concept with which they are trying to help their child. This is reflected in ISTE Standard 6a, which promotes fostering "a culture where students take ownership of their learning goals and outcomes in both independent and group settings" (ISTE, 2019b, para. 6).

Model coding

Coding is a wonderful — and productive — way to demonstrate to students that failure is inevitable. Work with students and learn from them as they begin to play with entry level coding. There are many online platforms to access this type of learning. Encourage students to share their successes and failures (teachers can also learn from the many student experiences along the way). By continually checking to see if their code does what they want it to, students will benefit from learning that failing frequently is often the path to success. Perfection from the beginning is unlikely, so those who try to build a "one-time perfect code" will learn that a lot of time and effort can be wasted by trying to avoid failure as a means of learning. They will quickly recognize that if they don't test their code frequently, their mistakes will compound. Facilitate and encourage conversations about how this might apply to other subjects or life-events. Allow them to make connections naturally to life outside of school so they can see how their work using technology applies in the real world. This can also help them reduce anxiety and become less fearful of making mistakes. ISTE standard 6d encourages us "to model and nurture creativity and creative expression to communicate ideas, knowledge, or connections" (ISTE, 2019b, para. 6).

Gamify your classroom

If you are thinking of utilizing games in your classroom, it's important to recognize that not all students like the same types of games. Some students like fast-paced, super-competitive games; others prefer creative building games; some choose mystery and adventure. To successfully plan and design appropriate tasks, it's important to spend time finding out why your students like certain types of games. A team of multidisciplinary researchers at the University of Waterloo have identified three basic video game player traits — action elements, aesthetic aspects, or goal oriented (EurekAlert, 2018, para. 1). This helps educators by tailoring the learning to student interests. In her article "Epic Fail or Win? Gamifying Learning in My Classroom," Liz Kolb suggests some simple ways to get started with game-based learning, including using online gamification software to help build quests, award points, and track student progress (Kolb, 2015, para. 3). The quests she uses are traditional tasks that are modified to be digital and can usually be completed in 10–25 min. For each quest completed, students are awarded points, with task complexity determining the number of points. Easier tasks would be awarded fewer points while complex tasks would be valued higher. These quests can be designed to unlock the next task or can be independent of each other. The key to the quests is to offer choice in allowing students to select their quests. Students are encouraged to collaborate with each other about their trials since, in the gaming world, failure is seen as power and not as weakness (Kolb, 2015, para. 12).

To encourage this concept, use a collaborative document so that students can screenshot and capture successes and failures to share with other people. This encourages students to reflect upon everything from strategy to mood/emotions, which works with any type of game. This empowers students to become less reluctant to take risks and encourages them to press on to complete the quest. Thus, it's important to design quests with an appropriate amount of failure built in. Students will be encouraged to learn from those failures and to make multiple attempts at success. Just remember not to make them so difficult that they knock students off their learning trajectory. According to ISTE standard 3b, we should "establish a learning culture that promotes curiosity and critical examination of online resources and fosters digital literacy and media fluency" (ISTE, 2019b, para. 3). Gamifying your classroom and critically examining game-based software allows us to promote curiosity and failure without fear.

Games as life models

Matthew Farber, Assistant Professor of Technology, Innovation, and Pedagogy, and author of *Gamify Your Classroom: A Field Guide to Game-Based Learning*, suggests that we use games to model what life was like thousands of years ago, how disease spreads globally, or how structures withstand natural and unnatural forces. Have students reflect on ways they could improve systems and models to better equip or support modern-day society, he says (Farber, 2016, para. 8). This allows the technology (or board game) to immerse students in spaces and thoughts that they may not otherwise have entered. This may also trigger curiosity and spark risk-taking in a way a student never thought was possible. ISTE standard 5c encourages us to "explore and apply instructional design principles to create innovative digital learning environments that engage and support learning" (ISTE, 2019b, para. 5).

Allow for sticky learning

It's really important that educators let go of some of the control and structure of a typical lesson. Students need time to discover tools — new software for example — so they can learn how to use them efficiently to leverage their learning. You can empower them by letting them be the teacher once they discover something new. Having students share with the class may, at times, look messy, but the messiness also allows students to become comfortable in developing their own individualized workflow. I strongly encourage students to use technology in small groups so they can learn from each other and feel more comfortable failing without being in front of the entire class. This provides time to develop their skills with their peers. ISTE Standard 6a suggests that we "foster a culture where students take ownership of their learning goals and outcomes in both independent and group settings" (ISTE, 2019b, para. 6).

Co-learn with students

A great way to overcome your own potential fear of failure with strategies or ideas you are unfamiliar with is to explore one of these new strategies together with your students. Of course, as the professional, you should set a goal and criteria for students to meet that goal, but then allow students to explore a new digital resource together. Allow students to become the experts and share with the class — and even teach you — when they discover something new, figure out a different way to perform a task, or ultimately achieve the overarching goal. After all, ISTE standard 4b urges us to "collaborate and co-learn with students" (ISTE, 2019b, para. 4). This could mean helping students troubleshoot a problem with technology so when they encounter a similar issue in future they will have the lived experience to solve the problem on their own. This may also mean helping them best identify what type of technology to use in certain situations and what platform or software they can use to demonstrate their learning. Doing this allows adults to learn from the children as well.

The reason I have discussed the ISTE standards so much is simple: as educators, we are preparing students for a future that we cannot yet imagine. Empowering students to become lifelong learners and providing them with the skills to face future challenges resourcefully and creatively is critical. It's not about using digital tools to support outdated education strategies and models; it's about tapping into technology's potential to amplify human capacity for collaboration, creativity, and communication. It's about levelling the playing field and providing young people with equitable access to powerful learning opportunities.

We are failing our students by simply sticking devices into their hands and assuming we are doing the right thing by "moving into the 21st century." We don't give children power tools without safety training, so it's equally dangerous to have children carelessly using technology. Instead, educators should use the ISTE standards to support classroom use of technology, reduce the fear of failure, and help students remove barriers in the way of their learning.

The ISTE frameworks and strategies are fantastic guidelines to help educators facilitate curriculum delivery. The time has clearly arrived for us to embrace new technology, so let's not let these resources languish like the professional development books that sit on library shelves collecting dust. We need to model risk-taking and learning at our students' level *with* them. When assistive technology first became a "thing," people didn't know what to think or do. Some thought it was cool, although not for them. Some thought it was a fad, like other things in education, that would come and go. Some thought it was outrageous and unfair for those who got to use it because they didn't have to work as hard. I vividly remember hearing a dismissive comment in the staffroom: "I'm not letting him use the part where he can talk to the computer. It will write it out for him. How is that fair to the other kids? It doesn't show me what he knows!" This comment still frustrates me to this day, although I'm smiling as I sit here using voice-to-text to write this book!

Ideas to try with colleagues or in the classroom

Using the idea of the "paradox of failure" — the clash between a player's desire to avoid failure and their drive to seek it out — have students reflect upon what they see as their deficiencies and then conference with them to compare their ideas with your own ideas for their improvement. Provide specific feedback as to how they can improve.

Share your personal goals for technology with your students. This will allow them to see that we are all working to get better and will empower them to overcome their fears around specific areas of learning.

What keeps you urgently optimistic? Journal or document what keeps you moving forward in education. Once a month, reflect on whether you are content with your optimism. Is it time to move on or do you still feel urgently optimistic about achieving your goals? This questioning will help to identify the barriers you may be facing and recognize whether they can be overcome.

Select one of the ISTE standards (https://www.iste.org/standards) and attempt to model its use in the next week. Document how it goes so you can reflect on this experience before you implement another standard.

Chapter 7

How Do Educators Manage Failure?

I can accept failure, everyone fails at something. But I can't accept not trying.

—Michael Jordan

I remember my first day of teaching as if it were yesterday. For that matter, I remember my first week, month, and even year! I mean how could you not? You feel like you've been thrown into the fire with no way out. I had a million and one questions about being all on my own in a classroom for the very first time. Much like parenting for the first time! It's that feeling you get when you leave the hospital and have no clue what you're really doing... so oblivious, yet determined to take on the challenge. I assumed that all the reading, studying, and classes of teachers' college would surely prepare me for both of these situations. I had that "Pfff, I don't need help with this... I got it!" attitude, and in both of those situations, I was so wrong. Learning to teach and learning to parent both come with plenty of questions, but at least with parenting you usually have a partner to bounce ideas off! First-year teachers have colleagues, of course, but how often do you want to run to them asking "Who's that?" "What is this form?" "What code?" "How do I teach reading?" "How many IEPs?" "What math concept do I start with?" "Why is this parent so upset... already?" Is this how it will be for the next 30 years?" — you get the idea.

Even more challenging is that, in addition to not wanting to pester your colleagues, you don't want them to think you aren't qualified. My resource teachers were amazing at offering to co-plan lessons, co-teach lessons, and help with assessments, but I was so sure I didn't need their help. I was a self-professed "expert in all domains" and I would simply respond with, "No thanks." These were 15-year veterans with a wealth of knowledge! Why did I turn them away? Fear of failure, actually. It is critical to break down our defense-mechanism barriers early in pre-service education programs, and encourage teachers to embrace support, take suggestions, ask questions — and not be afraid to make mistakes. We need to teach educators to expect failure and to embrace it as a necessary component of the learning process.

Educator Experiences

Nobody wants to be seen as a failure in front of their co-workers or peers. The fear, for me, was that veteran teachers would judge me as "doing it wrong." The truth is, I did not know how to assess properly, let alone how to teach properly, during my first year of teaching. Add to this stress the pressure that new teachers feel about not preparing kids properly for the next grade, and you have a problem about to implode.

Many new teachers suffer from what is known as "imposter syndrome." This phenomenon is not exclusive to the teaching profession; it afflicts anyone who feels like they are working or studying in a situation where everybody else belongs, but they do not deserve to be there. The syndrome is particularly acute, for example, in graduate school where students imagine that everyone else is smarter than they are. Imposter syndrome can also lead to people putting up barriers to create the illusion that they never make mistakes in a misguided attempt to fit in. Imposter syndrome is the main reason why new, and even experienced teachers, fear failing in front of their colleagues.

For some educators, there's also the fear of failing to be a good work colleague or the fear of not fitting in socially for reasons as wide-ranging as age, gender, race, sexual orientation, the extent to which you are an introvert or an extrovert, and even whether your opinions will conflict with those of the school community. I grew up as a student in a small farming community that would have struggled with having a teacher of colour or a different sexual orientation. Imagine the pressure such teachers would have felt in addition to the responsibility of delivering an impactful education.

Based on my own experiences, I asked new teachers about their early years of teaching. They said that there are many areas that they seek to improve, but classroom management and focusing on meeting the needs of all learners were clear priorities. The desire for best instructional practices was important, but not at the expense of trying to achieve early success. This makes sense for new teachers in the short term — after all, they're in survival mode!

Based on anecdotal evidence, when faced with adversity, most new teachers seem to turn to family for support. The most influential people that can help through tough times, however, are those on the administration team. Principals and vice-principals play an instrumental role in supporting new teachers on a daily basis. It is crucial for administrators to establish strong, meaningful relationships with all teachers, especially those just starting out. They need to know that the feeling of being a failure is common, but not to fear it since we grow by continuing to take risks as we learn to overcome adversity.

New Teacher Induction Program

In 2010, the Ontario government created the New Teacher Induction Program (NTIP) in order to support growth and professional development. NTIP provides new teachers with an additional year of support with a continuum of professional development to better equip them in the areas of assessment and effective teaching practices. By helping new teachers achieve their full potential, the NTIP also supports the vision of achieving high student performance. The document outlines the responsibilities for superintendents, principals, and mentors as well (Ontario Ministry of Education, 2010b, p. 3).

What Can New Educators Do to Manage Failure?

Think Positively

First, educate yourself about the importance of a positive mindset. Be open to new ideas. What was taught in pre-service won't necessarily work in every scenario.

It's frustrating to see students who will not engage in learning or wrestle with a challenging concept because they desperately want to protect their own self-worth and pride and will do so at any cost. We need to remind ourselves that, as educators, we must avoid this impulse too. We can't always be right, and we need to stop investing our time in trying to preserve a self-image based on always being right. As you grow as an educator, learning to overcome a fear of failure early in your career will be one of the most critical things you can model for your students.

This is why it is so important to model positive thinking in our classrooms and use speak alouds as we work through something challenging. By doing this, we help students visualize how they can move from a fixed mindset to challenge themselves in positive ways. We need to show them that by being vulnerable, we naturally become stronger and become able to handle challenging situations in a positive way that allows us to grow.

We all need constructive feedback in order to grow. When giving yours, use protocols and student work samples to allow you to dialogue purposefully or to narrow your focus. When communicating with students, making the focus about evidence in their work is always productive and avoids personal attacks and getting off topic. For more ideas, check out *Collaborative Inquiry for Educators: A Facilitator's Guide to School Improvement* by Jenni Donohoo.

Select a Mentor

Speaking of constructive feedback, having a mentor is more important than most people realize, including me when I was starting out. Leaning on a mentor — another person to bounce ideas off and learn from — would have helped me immensely. The ideal approach isn't simply to choose someone you enjoy chatting with; a good mentor is much more than that. A mentor chosen simply based on their years of experience or an administrator's suggestion could end up being worse than having no mentor at all. Informally interview your prospective candidates. Find out if they have the time and inclination to mentor you. Good training for mentors would also be beneficial. To get the most value out of a mentor–mentee relationship, it shouldn't be short-term; a 5–7 year commitment would be ideal.

Mentors have a duty not only to be available to their mentee in a responsive role; they also need to be engaged proactively. A rich curriculum-delivery methodology and pedagogy, for example, can help manage behavioural issues. An interesting, meaningful, purposeful lesson — in the eyes of the student — is a key part of classroom management in reducing behavioural outbursts. Mentors can play a critical role in helping to design such lessons, and there are plenty of resources to support teachers in this area. *Beyond Monet: The Artful Science of Instructional Integration* by Barry Bennett and Carol Rolheiser is a favourite of mine.

Teaching strategies naturally grow in complexity as you become more self-confident and as your relationship with your school and your administration team grows. If your administrator isn't visible in your classroom, invite them in. Inform them of your goals — especially as they change — so they can monitor your progress and support you where necessary. Ensure that your goals align with your school and board improvement plan and districts goals. After all, your principal might end up becoming your mentor, especially in a small school or school board. Do what you can to get to know them personally. Ask them questions about their family, what they like to do outside of school, what bumps along the road they have experienced to help you avoid them. In other words, build that relationship.

Open Communication with Your Mentor

Establish open lines of communication between yourself and your mentor. Technology has facilitated this, so make it rich and intentional. Be sure to document the areas of growth that BOTH of you are working on. This isn't a one-way street. Seek out key information related to how to know that students are learning, being able to determine if something you do isn't working and exploring what would happen if something changed.

Ask that your mentor's support be tailored to you; be assertive and respectful as to what you need. Once you've established this, set up protocols and a plan to achieve specifically what you feel you need. If you would like support with giving students timely and effective feedback, ask for manageable and efficient support. If you need to see how to give ongoing feedback as part of your daily flow, ask your mentor to coach you. If you need excellent resources, ask for them. If your mentor is pushing you too quickly, tell them. If it's too slow, mention it. Mentoring is not a one-size-fits-all approach, so shape it for your own needs.

Take risks and expect chaos. Be clear also about what your limits are for failure. Everyone has a different threshold for risk-taking and failure. Anticipate what might go wrong with your mentor and be prepared to respond in a flexible manner. By preparing yourself to expect a certain level of chaos, you prepare yourself for the fall and allow yourself permission to reflect on the situation or failure, and then try it again. This level of planning will also allow you to be intentional about teaching students to overcome their fears of failure.

Start to think about a long-range exit strategy with your mentor. This is a productive, semi-long-term relationship of perhaps 5–7 years. At some point, it will make sense to move forward on your own. Pay attention to how the mentor–mentee relationship is working. If you aren't getting the support you need, have the confidence to engage in that challenging conversation. If it doesn't change satisfactorily, then part ways professionally. You will no doubt continue to lean on them for other areas where they can offer support.

Ideas to Support Yourself

All the mentorship in the world does not take the onus off you to pay attention to your own needs and growth. Here are some ideas for self-care.

Expand Your Network

Expand your network by one person a month. Technology has brought all educators closer, so find like-minded people who are curious about the same initiatives as you. Pick their brains about what works for them in their country, culture, and classroom. Such networking can also lead to some interesting co-operative projects that can expand your classroom beyond its own walls.

Exercise

Exercise for at least 15 minutes, three times a week. This could be during your lunch if you have a crazy household like mine. Even better than exercising alone, start a running club with the students or take on coaching an after-school team to encourage them to stay physically fit and active. Anything physical that elevates the heart rate is good cardio-vascular exercise. This type of "outdoor Ed" will help to both reduce behaviour problems in the class and build a better rapport with your students. Use this time to talk with them about what makes them tick and what their interests are. This will pay off in the long run. A healthy body promotes a healthy mind.

Be Reflective

Reflection is an undervalued step in your journey. Teaching can be overwhelming, so make sure you take some time to step back and reflect on all the positive changes that you've made happen. You've chosen the perfect career to become a life-long learner, so keep moving forward!

What Can All Educators Do to Manage Failure?

Reduce the Urge for Perfection

Despite knowing that it's impossible to be perfect, considering all the complexities involved in being an educator, we always pressure ourselves to be the best we can be. Fear of failure is often pinpointed as a primary motivation underlying perfectionism (Conroy, Kaye, & Fifer, 2007, p. 238). Perfectionism means setting standards that are too high to achieve, which leaves people feeling like they can't attain their goals

(Hewitt & Flett, 1991, p. 238). If we can recognize the areas that elicit fear of failure in our day-to-day work, we can begin to defuse it. Ask the people around you what *their* realistic expectations of you are. You will most likely find that their expectations aren't as high as you may have thought. Openly communicating with people around you will help defuse self-oriented perfectionism. Ask people around you what they think *your* expectations are. Start small by asking them what they think your expectations are regarding the outcome of one specific lesson. Compare what they believe is a realistic outcome with your intended outcome, and be willing to readjust your expectations.

Admit to Failure

Remember that it's okay to fail; relieve that pressure of trying to achieve perfection. Maintain high standards for yourself without being unrealistic. When mistakes happen, don't pretend they didn't; mention the mistakes in conversations with students or colleagues. It's important to identify both why it happened (unprepared, didn't predict possible outcomes, something was out of your control, you set unrealistic expectations, etc.) *and* what you will do differently to prevent it from happening again. Choose a time frame for trying again, but keep it short. Retry whatever went wrong within a day or two, otherwise you lose your momentum. Don't let the mistakes define you, however. It's crucial to acknowledge and celebrate your daily successes.

Develop Self-Awareness

Allow yourself time and space to develop self-awareness regarding the effects of stress and exposure to failure. Understand that before teachers can approach their students and begin to apply resilience-building activities within their own classrooms, they need to spend some time identifying their own strengths and weaknesses and building personal resources (Baum, 2005, p. 495). Design lessons that develop self-esteem, develop coping strategies, and create social supports, hope, meaning, optimism, and humor. Doing this with students allows both them and you to find hope and meaning in difficult situations.

Be Mindful of Mindfulness

Incorporating mindfulness into your teaching allows you to better connect with your students on a personal level. This helps you to reduce their level of stress towards education and allows you to avoid the burnout that could lead you to leaving the profession (Killoran & Bliss, 2017, p. 99). In her 2015 article "Seven Ways Mindfulness Can Help Teachers," Patricia Jennings, an internationally recognized leader in mindfulness in education, acknowledges that mindfulness can include deep breathing and relaxation, but it also involves consciously training our minds to become more aware of our inner and outer experiences, as well as learning how to manage our emotions. Her insight, coupled with my own experiences, resulted in this list of ways that developing mindfulness can help us be better educators.

1. **Be aware of emotions.** We spend so much time thinking about and planning our lessons that we sometimes lose sight of the emotions running through our classrooms. By practicing mindfulness, we can consciously train our brain to be aware of the emotional peaks and valleys both within ourselves and within our students (Jennings, 2015, para. 8).

2. **Communicate clearly.** Often we send mixed messages to students by asking questions at the end of a sentence like, "You understood that, right?" This implies that students should respond. If you weren't anticipating a response, this could frustrate you. By being more mindful of our words, we can avoid confusion and frustration (Jennings, 2015, para 10).

3. **Manage the students you find difficult.** Practicing mindfulness allows us to understand what each student needs and what triggers certain behaviours. Rather than reacting negatively to a student who is constantly fidgeting or who speaks out after listening to you for 20–30 minutes, look at it from their perspective. It's not easy to sit and listen for that amount of time (Jennings, 2015, para 13).

4. **Set up a positive learning environment.** We can foster a good learning environment by incorporating student opinions,

monitoring how we respond to students, controlling our tone of voice and body language, and setting up our physical classroom space in a productive way. Be mindful of student needs and plan your layout, lighting, textures, walls, and resources accordingly (Jennings, 2015, para 18).

a. **Student voice.** Ask students for their input during the first days and weeks on everything from classroom expectations to seating arrangements and the look and feel of the classroom environment. By doing this, you get better buy in and student ownership of how their year will go. By explaining that you will honour their voices, you set them up to expect to contribute *and* to be heard. You still sift through all that input to make the final decisions as to what will work best for the entire class.

b. **Listening and responding.** It's critical that we give students undivided attention when we are listening to them. We cannot be on our phones, looking elsewhere, or speaking to another child if we truly value their input. Our body language needs to convey that we are ready to listen, our eyes need to make contact with the speaker (unless they tell us or their cultural background suggests otherwise), and we need to be asking clarifying questions to demonstrate that we fully understand them. While doing this, our tone of voice needs to demonstrate enthusiasm and curiosity. At times, our sense of humour and "poking fun" can shut down an idea and tell a child that we don't value their ideas or creativity. Allow your tone of voice, your posture, and your smile to keep kids communicating. After all, their ideas and creativity can change the world!

c. **Physical layout.** Get to know the learners who are going to occupy the space. Every learner is different; some have more needs, some require physical accessibility, others demand more intellectually. Your physical space should provide a seamless transition between you the teacher and what your learners need to help them be successful. Your walls need to provide another support network to extend learning and reinforce basic concepts that students can revisit. If you value reflective thinking and conversation as part of the learning process, then having children sitting in rows is actively working against you. If you have learners who need to stand and stretch but you have not defined a way for them to do this, then your environment isn't reflecting your ideology. If you have defined spaces or tools that students need to access independently, then teach them how to interact with them or it will lead to frustration and confusion. Once your students are familiar with your physical space, take time to reflect to ensure that your environment supports your philosophy.

d. **How about you?** Greet each child, each morning at the door with a smile and a welcome. This small gesture tells each child that you see them and care about them. Over time, this will naturally build trust. It also allows you to see who needs more attention or who isn't having the greatest start to their day. It's tough to take risks and fail without fear when you're not feeling included and ready to learn. Think about the resources that you need to optimize your teaching and their learning (both physical and virtual). Be their biggest cheerleaders, contact their parents frequently with positive news, and speak to them outside of class time to find out what their true passions are. These gestures will bear fruit as the year progresses.

5. **Strengthen your relationships.** Give each student full, mindful attention in short spurts to demonstrate that you see and hear them. This intentional, quality attention will establish strong student–teacher relationships and create a strong sense of community. As you get comfortable with your class and students, schedule one-on-one conferencing time in your daily schedule

so you can get to know your students even better. This is a great time to set individual goals with your students and share your goals too. This process allows students to see that you value setting and reaching goals. As these conferences progress, your feedback regarding their goals will help propel them forward. Students watch and look up to you. They want support tailored to their own individual needs, not a one-size-fits-all approach. Taking the time to speak and actively listen to your students will naturally shape your program and its delivery.

6. **Slow down.** We tend to get caught up in "covering" the curriculum and getting through our planned lessons. In doing so, we sometimes lose the feel for what's going on around us and who needs what. Students process information at different speeds, so by slowing down and taking a mindful moment during a lesson, you become more aware of both your flow and your students' flow, creating a more symbiotic, harmonious learning pace.

7. **Build community.** We all desire a sense of belonging and wanting to give back. We can cultivate this by modelling caring routines within our classroom. Examples of this include checking in with each student before they enter the class, smiling at each other, holding the door for someone, complimenting one another, using a calm voice, active listening, and generally helping and caring for each other (Jennings, 2015). By starting to build a strong sense of community in our classroom, we can move students towards extending that community within the school and eventually into the greater community.

Ideas to try with colleagues or in the classroom

Be open about sharing failed experiences and treating them as an opportunity to grow. Document what helped you and what you learned. This same strategy can be used with students. Here's an example:

My Failures	What did I learn?	What helped me through it?
Today my math lesson flopped and my students failed to understand the concept of 10.	I presumed they had enough background knowledge with using base ten blocks to demonstrate composing and decomposing the number.	I communicated this to my teaching partner and administrator. They suggested that I spend time teaching my students how to use the manipulatives ahead of time so they could better use them independently.

Get a "teaching buddy" and sit in each other's classroom during your planning time. Be intentional about what you want to see. Transitional times? Positive reward systems? Small-group instructions? Questions being asked? By being intentional and goal-oriented when you do an observation, you allow yourself to better focus. For example, you may ask a teaching partner, "Can I come to your class to see how you transition from whole class instruction to your guided reading groups?"

Film or record each other and analyze the results. This requires a strong level of trust. If you take the risk and make this happen early in the year, the payoff will be huge. Be sure to identify one or two things that you are looking to improve, and only reflect on those areas so that the exercise does not become overwhelming. I once recorded myself to listen for how often I asked open-ended questions versus closed questions during math class. Surprisingly, I asked many closed questions that didn't require a great deal of thought, like, "You understand that right?" and "Hands up if this makes sense to you." This reflective process changed how I used questioning in my practice. I started carrying a variety of different questions (representing, comparing, etc.) on a keyring so that I could improve my repertoire to encourage deeper thinking.

Chapter 8

Instructional Strategies: How to Rock Your Teaching Practices and Your Students' Worlds

"It is fine to celebrate success, but it is more important to heed the lessons of failure."

—Bill Gates

A book simply discussing the concept of failing without fear, and the importance of embracing failure as a way forward in learning, will only take us — as educators — so far. We need to be able to implement ideas as we shift our approach to work toward student success. The primary focus of this final chapter is to examine more strategies to best support your learners, schools, and systems in an effort to banish the fear of failure.

Connecting the Dots

As you reflect on the ideas and material in this book, it's important to take your new — or reaffirmed — thoughts and determine the applicable action steps. These next series of strategies are key in building momentum as you ultimately move closer to fostering students who embrace failure without fear. The order in which you chose to implement the following steps will depend upon your entry point (both the phase of the school year and your readiness to jump in) and your students' entry point in getting to know you:

- Empower your learners
- Create a responsive environment
- Know your curriculum
- Ask effective questions
- Make assessment transparent
- Promote risk-taking

As you implement these strategies, continue to question what works best. This will allow you to engage in a natural inquiry process in how you work with your students to eliminate what doesn't work and become more intentional and focused on what does (Hannay, Wideman, & Seller, 2010). When anchored in student voice, the work we do in our classrooms and schools naturally becomes the grassroots research that helps us identify gaps and strengths so that we can move closer to our desired outcomes. After all, it is the students who can tell us what urgent learning is needed. The only way we can do this, and lead our students to believe in failure without fear, is by getting to know them as best as we possibly can.

Empower Your Learners

In order to help students develop a positive and flexible mindset, it is essential that you get to know your learners. If you don't know how your students think, it is impossible to design lessons and units that meet them where their interests and ability levels are. By using interest surveys, and communicating with parents or guardians, you can learn what motivates each child to succeed. Once we have that information, our professional knowledge and experience can guide us to find the best approach for each student so they feel empowered. Empowering students takes time and requires building trust with students so they feel a deep sense of belonging. Dr. Robyne Hanley-Dafoe, a psychology and education instructor at Trent University in Ontario, reminds us that we all want to feel a sense of belonging and to have a meaningful purpose. This helps reduce stress levels in students, allowing them to feel part of a team (Hanley-Dafoe, 2019, para 3). One way to empower students is to use student-centred surveys that ask what they are good at, what they are passionate about, who the important people in their lives are, what their interests are outside of school, what worries them, and what they are fearful of. The next step is to survey their parents and ask the same questions. This creates opportunities to engage in meaningful conversations with students, all centred around them, creating a sense of empowerment.

I once had a very difficult, even intimidating, Grade 6 student who constantly acted out, wouldn't listen, challenged every decision, and generally didn't like school. This particular situation was a personal challenge, especially given that this child was already negatively labelled — in some cases even written off — as a typical badass student. I made it my goal to speak with him outside of class about anything *but* school-related topics. I learned to let go of his... colourful... language, and through these ongoing conversations, he mentioned often that he spent time with his grandpa, and that he really looked up to him. I decided to call his grandpa one day to ask him what his grandson valued and how he managed his behaviour when things were heading south. He was shocked that a teacher had reached out to him and mentioned that this had never happened before. He told me a story about trust, belonging, and empowerment.

He said, "Chad, he needs to not only feel trusted; he needs to know deep down that you care and will continue to trust him even when he's at his worst." He continued, "One day when he's going off, give him your car keys, and ask him to go get something for you." I wasn't sure what to make of this and wasn't about to take this wild advice but continued to listen. "You need to trust that he won't steal or drive your car. If you trust him, he'll trust you. He's not a bad kid and doesn't want to behave this way; he just doesn't know how to manage himself and doesn't know how to fill the 'bad kid' void he has created if he doesn't have that persona attached to him." This made perfect sense, and that conversation helped immensely. The following day, this student was having another gem of a day, so I decided to do the unthinkable. I gave him my car keys and asked him to go get my lunch — I mysteriously had "forgotten" it in my car. From that day forward our relationship changed for the better, and we went on to have a great year. My message isn't to give students your car keys; in fact, I would avoid that! My message is to think outside of the box regarding ways you can connect with each student in your class to help them feel trusted and capable. This will empower students to do great things — even fail without fear.

Create a Responsive Environment

Ideally, we all create responsive space while in a regulated state for our students. According to the Northeast Foundation for Children (2019), the Responsive Classroom approach emphasizes social, emotional, and academic growth to foster a strong and safe school community, based on the following six guiding principles:

1. **Teaching social and emotional skills is as important as teaching academic content.** A practical way to do this is to examine the learning skills portion of your official curriculum document, and break that language down into student-friendly language. By doing this, you can set goals specific to the social side of teaching so that students know what to expect and what they are aiming for. The same can be done with emotional regulation. It is key to teach what emotions look like and feel like at different ages and how to reset to be ready to learn. This might mean having a toolkit containing a variety of calming tools to help regulate the mind and body such as stress balls, sensory sand, noise cancelling headphones, colouring activities, or music. Creating a "calming" corner in the classroom offers a physical space dedicated to students who need less hectic surroundings. These could be tent-like, covered spaces or have privacy screens. Besides the contents of the toolkit, the calming corner might contain books to read, a compression blanket, and cards to guide the student through deep breathing or other meditative exercises. For students who need physical activity, a

"busy" corner with an exercise bike or posters on activities like wall-sits, jumping jacks, hops, or push-ups might be helpful. Of course, we need to teach students how to use these spaces, otherwise they won't be able to engage in productive emotional regulation.

2. **How we teach is as important as what we teach.** Reflect on your teaching style. If your space is visually busy and overwhelming, is it fair to students who have sensory issues? If your program is primarily based on sitting and working for sixty minutes and beyond, is that suitable for students who struggle to focus? A great way to know if your teaching style is in tune with how your students function best is to simply ask them through conferencing or surveys. Don't take the results personally if they aren't to your liking. If you truly value a responsive space, you will respond accordingly to the needs of your students.

3. **Great cognitive growth occurs through social interaction.** Engage in conversations with students about their interests outside of the classroom. They really do look up to you and want to tell you, so just ask them. Social interaction also means peer-to-peer opportunities. Students learn just as much from each other as they do from you, so we need to create the conditions for positive and productive conversations in our classrooms. This can be done by creating a series of "We will…" commitment statements for the class. Here are some that I've used:

    a. We will positively add to each other's ideas
    b. We will be optimistic that we can find a solution
    c. We will respectfully challenge each other's ideas
    d. We will make mistakes and learn from them

4. **What we know and believe about our students — individually, culturally, developmentally — informs our expectations, reactions, and attitudes about them.** Keep the bar high. It's our professional obligation to be responsive to any gender identity, cultural background, exceptionality, or belief, but this

doesn't mean we need to lower the bar. Working within these parameters, we adapt our practice to support all students by raising the floor *and* pushing on the ceiling. Do your homework: seek out resources you need to understand every learner in your classroom so that you can maximize their potential.

5. **How we work together as adults to create a safe, joyful, inclusive school environment is as important as our individual contributions or competences.** Remember that you are one person in a sea of many. You can't do this work on your own. It's important to reach out and ask for help when you need ideas, support, or resources so that you can remain healthy in order to lead others, to activate the team around you. Most of the time, we think of the adults, but we can also engage the students to let us know how to bring joy and inclusivity to them. Ask for ideas about what they would add to or take away from your class to make it a better environment.

6. **Partnering with families — getting to know them and valuing their contributions — is as important as knowing the children we teach.** Reaching out to families is a great way to enrich your program and your environment. This can be done by introducing the idea of "ask an expert" so that parents can speak to the class. Link these talks with curriculum units through the year so that you constantly have "experts" joining your classroom, creating a sense of belonging for them also.

Student voice should be included as much as possible to create a positive and productive space. We need to ensure that students have proper sight lines, are free from as many distractions as possible, and are sitting or standing in a location that works for them.

When I worked in a Kindergarten to Grade 8 school in a rural location, my classroom had huge windows overlooking the fields that our students played in. One of my Grade 3 students was having a tough day. He was stuck but wasn't using any of the support materials on the walls — success criteria, anchor charts, and a math word wall. I asked him why not. His response was puzzling: "Well, I have no clue why she 'plasticed' those darn things because all I see are the goalposts and I just want to go out and play soccer." I wasn't sure how "plasticed" or "goalposts" came into this conversation, so I replied, "Tell me more, I'm a bit confused."

"I'll never pass this assignment this way. If you come down here to my level Mr. Reay, the sun shines off the *plasticed* posters and the reflection is of the goalposts outside."

"Oh, that makes sense to me now," I replied. "I think the word you were looking for was 'laminated,' but either way, let's come up with a plan."

This path forward all came from simply asking the student about his experience. This student might never have mentioned the issue about glare from the sun, so it is a great reminder of something that seems small, but can have a huge impact on student achievement. I had worked with this student and earned his trust; otherwise, he would have never opened up to me. Using his insight into this distraction, we were able to come up with a solution. We agreed to make personal versions of the posters for him and for a few others who needed them.

Besides the classroom teacher, support staff (Educational Assistants, Teacher Assistants) also need to be checking in throughout each day to make sure that students have the optimal learning environment. This proactive, rather than reactive, approach helps us avoid classroom misbehaviour or impaired learning due to simple lack of focus. Besides the "calming" and "busy" corners, all students may benefit from reduced lighting, assistive technology, carpets, blankets, and incorporating calming activities such as yoga. If the environment changes to a field trip, assembly, or outdoor location, work to adapt as many of these accommodations as possible to the new environment. Remember to plan trips and other activities by keeping struggling students in the forefront.

Know Your Curriculum

The ability to take risks effectively with your students requires having a solid grasp of the curriculum you are teaching. You need to know what concepts build on one another as children become developmentally ready for new information. How do the specific expectations support the big ideas? How can you integrate certain concepts from one aspect of the curriculum with ideas from another to promote rich, authentic experiences that elicit learning? How can you make all this unfold, like a beautiful dance, all while balancing the assessment that informs your next steps? Obviously, this doesn't come easily. It requires intentionality, experience, reflection, and feedback to make it all come together. The failure without fear concept comes in to play when you give yourself permission — specifically once you are the expert in your curriculum — to take risks and be bold in your delivery. This promotes growth in yourself, and ultimately in your students. As they see you modelling risk-taking, they benefit from the opportunities you provide.

It is okay to check — and double and triple check for that matter — the expectations of the curriculum while planning or co-planning. Often unit plans start with an idea someone has based on an existing unit. But just because a unit sounds amazing, full of "cool" activities, doesn't mean it's aligned with the curriculum, or is the best way to leverage learning, promote risk taking and positive failure, and foster learning with a strong student interest. Once when I was team-teaching, an experienced teacher handed me a series of lessons and assured me, "It will be amazing. The whole class will love it, and we could even do a whole division or school inquiry about this!" Although I loved the enthusiasm and internal drive, I mentioned that this "topic" didn't appear anywhere in the current curriculum. The response I got was, "It must be because I've been teaching this unit for 15 years." The curriculum had changed; unfortunately, the lesson had not. Teaching outdated information, or using outdated approaches, is another example of setting students up for negative failure. The stakes could range from not being prepared for the next grade to not learning what they need to know to navigate society successfully. If you find yourself in this situation, don't make it personal. Have the confidence to simply refer yourself and your colleagues to your guiding documents and ask, "Where does this best align with the curriculum, and what other areas or subjects can I/we include to make this a rich experience for children?"

Ask Effective Questions

Questions make up a huge part of our day, both as parents and as educators. Steven Hastings, from the *Times Educational Supplement* (TES), a weekly UK publication aimed primarily at schoolteachers, suggests that educators ask approximately 400 questions a day, depending on the age group of their students. His research shows that educators ask up to two questions every minute, around 70 thousand a year, or two to three million in the course of a career. Questioning accounts for up to a third of all teaching time with most questions answered in less than a second. His research has found that increasing the wait time after asking a question improves the number and quality of responses from students, the ideal time being three seconds for a lower-order question and more than 10 seconds for a higher-order question (Hastings, 2003, p. 1).

We need to give our students that cognitive space in our instructional practice. We need to let them know that it's good to take time to think about an answer and that it's still okay to get it wrong. We also need to encourage our students to ask more questions. Research by The Right Question Institute in Boston indicates that student questioning drops off massively once children begin formal education. Preschool students ask their parents an average of 100 questions a day, yet by middle school they've virtually stopped asking questions, as Figure 8.1 shows.

Why does kids' questioning drop off after age 3?

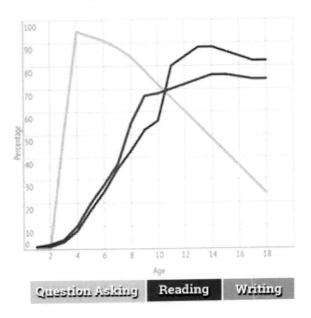

Figure 8.1 (Source: Berger, n.d.)

Knowing this, why not make our questions more meaningful, more purposeful? Stop asking yes/no questions that can easily be shrugged off or looked up, and start asking questions that force problem solving as opposed to recall. This will help us all promote deeper thought processes. Be intentionally inclusive when questioning students. Instead of asking the same students who always know the answer, or answering the question yourself, ask your way through your entire class. Remember to slow down; children need time to think and articulate their thoughts. A good way to monitor your questioning skills is to record yourself. When I listened to myself, I realized that my go-to line was, "You got this right?" I shifted my practice because the students were simply nodding yes, even when I knew they did not understand certain concepts.

The Ontario Ministry of Education has released some wonderful monographs about supporting teachers with asking effective questions. In their Capacity Building Series, the publication "Asking Effective Questions" makes several suggestions:

- Anticipate your students' thoughts and questions.
- Use learning goals to frame your questions. Learning goals are the foundation of your lessons, so connect the two.
- Ask open-ended questions: "How would it work if you changed…?" or "Tell me more about…?"
- Ask questions that require an answer. Rhetorical questions don't promote meaningful thought.
- Use verbs that elicit higher levels of thinking, reflection, and synthesizing. (Ontario Ministry of Education, 2011)

The monograph also does a nice job of breaking questions down into sections to help students:

- think about
- share their representations
- reflect on their work
- make connections
- share their feelings, attitudes, and beliefs
- reflect
- invent and problem solve

Asking effective questions means allowing students time to think, process, and share their thinking. "Turn and talk" and "think-pair-share" are two strategies to increase the level of thought in your classroom.

Turn and Talk

Imagine standing at the front of the room and delivering a masterful lesson. Suddenly you hear chitter-chatter; your immediate reaction might be to become offended. Your next reaction is probably to ask the students to stop talking. It's possible they are talking about something entirely unrelated; however, it's also possible that they have ideas about the material that they want to explore. Perhaps they actually want to talk and contribute, and we get in their way because we want to get through the curriculum. In these moments, a quick 30-second "turn and talk" is the perfect strategy. Allow students the opportunity for relevant, accountable talk and really turn learning loose. Don't squash it — foster it. Let students share their knowledge. This is a great opportunity to address misconceptions and build on prior knowledge.

Think-Pair-Share

Don't forget the "think" part of this strategy. All too often, we jump right to the pair and share aspect. We need to give students time to formulate their own thoughts about the learning process or the material. This is when students will be able to mentally prepare or consolidate what they think and are willing to share. Especially for identified students, English Language Learners, or reluctant students, sharing with a partner provides a safe opportunity to orally rehearse a response, and listen to someone else's response. If the teacher calls upon them, they can share their own ideas *or* ideas from their partner. This is a simple way to promote and support risk-taking. As one student said, "My confidence to publicly speak in my own classroom shot through the roof, and I quickly realized that even if I make a mistake it's no big deal. I realized that as I started to share and become more confident that I wasn't the only one making mistakes and that I was actually learning more about myself as well as the subject." This student was learning to fail without fear.

Make Assessment Transparent

Education systems need to do a better job of incorporating failure as part of assessment practices. We need to share assessment information with children through a different lens; one that helps students to fail, learn, and grow, all while linking the process to everyday life. This may mean zooming out to look holistically at how we implement and execute our assessment practices. As teachers, we determine student success or failure by arbitrarily giving grades, and in doing so, we often marginalize certain students, effectively setting them up for failure outside of school as well. In the true concept of learning, however, nobody fails. What if children started a movement demanding the opportunity to struggle without being deemed failures? What if they all identified themselves as strong, capable learners wishing to be taught/coached based specifically on their individual needs and then evaluated in a non-comparative way? What if students challenged us to deliver modern programs leveraged with technology support? These questions lead to a new approach, perhaps one in which students start to push for a system that teaches to each student and not to the masses. This will be met with resistance and will take time, but it is worthy of our consideration. We also need to be cognizant of how it would change pre-service teaching institutions, which would be a great starting point for a new attitude toward failing without fear.

Diagnostic assessments are often used without individual intention and more like a one-size-fits-all model. The idea is to use a diagnostic assessment to gauge where a student's learning is at in order to help determine an appropriate entry point for instruction. This type of diagnostic tool must include components where students can demonstrate their thinking process, as well as feedback capacity for comments about where they got stuck, what strategies they tried, and what would help them moving forward. The assessment needs to allow for questions back to the educator, enabling students to highlight key information about what they are still struggling with. These additions to a standard diagnostic tool will lead to productive failure. A good diagnostic will have the aforementioned areas of reflection, but also include knowledge and understanding, thinking, and application-type questions. A fair cross-section and variety of questions will help teachers determine — accurately and quickly — how to help a child learn forward. This cannot be done through a traditional worksheet. Through observational, conversational, and statistical data, we can better triangulate to determine what was happening when a student wasn't successful. If students are able to complete a diagnostic assessment without any sort of struggle, we haven't pushed that child to the maximum of their academic rigour. If we continue to give students superficial knowledge and ask questions that don't probe their understanding of ideas or concepts, we don't allow any opportunity for students to ask deep questions, think critically, and have the opportunity to struggle through the process of learning; we are not allowing students to exceed their mental capacity and to grow as individuals.

The academic information that diagnostic assessments give us will help us to plan lessons and units that hit each child's zone of proximal development, pushing them beyond it. Without this information, we run the risk of planning tasks that are too easy and don't promote risk-taking or provide any opportunity for failure. We also run the risk of planning tasks that are too difficult, which can cause students to shut down and not attack the task with an open mind.

Grant Wiggins, president of Authentic Education in Hopewell, New Jersey, claims that you don't need any "teaching"; you only need a good feedback system (Wiggins, 2012). As painful as it might be for us educators to realize, it's not necessarily teaching that causes learning. Wiggins refers to Eric Mazur, a Harvard physics professor who is a proponent of the idea that "less teaching + more feedback = better learning." This implies that learners need more time doing, attempting, and trying and less time being "taught." This also means that educators need to be giving constant meaningful feedback based on output rather than spend the majority of their time front-loading students with information. The key take-away is that good lesson design is critical to optimizing the opportunity to provide twice as much feedback as direct instruction. Formal teaching plays a minor role in a well-designed learning environment.

In his article "Seven Keys to Effective Feedback," Wiggins (2012) suggests that helpful feedback is

1. Goal-referenced
2. Tangible and transparent
3. Actionable
4. User-friendly (specific and personalized)
5. Timely
6. Ongoing
7. Consistent

Educators need to pivot and shift towards becoming learning coaches by giving personalized feedback, providing social and emotional support to clarify students' visions, and helping them turn those visions into realty in order to promote lifelong learners.

This poses an even bigger question. Could we evolve to a system without marks or grades? By moving more towards a mastery-based approach with personalized, detailed, timely feedback along the way, we remove the pressure of performing for the grade. I know educators who have moved in this direction found it liberating for them *and* their students. This means that we abandon neither planning nor learning outcomes. In fact, it raises the bar because the focus is on mastery of a concept, not simply learning it during a set time as determined by the teacher.

Districts within British Columbia, as well as other schools and districts across the country, are implementing this concept. Peter Jory, director of instruction, technology, and innovation for the Sea to Sky school district, told CBC's *The Early Edition* that students would receive report cards with detailed feedback and "remove the distraction of the letter grade. [We've found] when they see the letter grade, they disregard everything after that," Jory said. "The thing that we're concerned about here is that students associate themselves with the grade that they receive. Students who receive a C– associate themselves with that, and are prone to switch off. [...] Conversely, students who receive an A try to protect themselves, and work towards that A, rather than doing more challenging, meaningful tasks. We're finding some of our highest achieving students are really good at gaming the system. If we produce confident, adaptable learners who are interested in what they are pursuing, they're going to do really well regardless of how they're assessed" (Nair, 2017).

My own experience as a student reflects this approach. After all, an A never made me a better artist, but making mistakes and getting timely and constructive feedback along the way sure helped. This approach can be a tough one for parents to get their heads around, so if you choose to move in this direction, be sure that it is a school-based decision with support from your administrative team and clearly laid out and explained to parents from the beginning of the year.

Criteria for Positive Failure

The phrase "success criteria" encourages students to be just that: successful. Determining what it means to be successful is of course important, but the very notion of "success criteria" seems to preclude failure. It would be interesting — and beneficial — if we spent time with students unpacking the criteria for them to respect failure, not fear it. This would help students understand that failure is normal and what it means to fail successfully and productively as part of a learning process. Including failure as part of success could be viewed as negative, but it's the exact opposite. When we constantly tell students that learning is about being successful, we put a lot of stress on them not to fail. When failure does happen — as it invariably does — students feel constricted to follow the step-by-step procedures (often listed in the success criteria) and are less likely to take risks and be creative. This is when the mental health of students starts to become at risk. If they are not successful — in the eyes of their teacher — they may no longer see themselves reflected in the school culture. If that happens and they become disengaged, they become difficult to re-engage, and may therefore exit our education system early. We need to create and seize opportunities to teach, model, and demonstrate to children how others struggle and fail before they struggle and succeed. We need to share with students our own experiences in overcoming failure and embracing mistakes. Dealing with failure might actually be the most important thing we can teach them.

Dealing with failure teaches you to believe in yourself and your own coping abilities. If you believe in yourself, you will have the confidence to fail and not feel judged by it. Insecure people fear being judged for making mistakes and eventually end up hiding their successes as well. Self-reflection will keep you grounded and focused on your students' needs. Often people feel like underachievers in their own lives, especially when compared to the air-brushed lives on social media. Are you guilty of letting other people dictate how you feel about yourself? Are you guilty of presenting biased or misleading information that could negatively affect someone else?

Promote Risk-Taking

We can't promote risk-taking for students of all ability levels and then punish those who don't get it right the first time by giving them poor grades. This halts the process of innovation. We can't provide greater autonomy but then get frustrated at how long it takes them to meet a specific definition of success, either regarding the curriculum material or their behaviour. Instead, we must teach students specific strategies so they become active participants in their own emotional regulation and behaviour. There is no better resilience builder than helping a student better understand their own emotions and how to control them.

Risky Business

Ask students what risks they feel they have recently taken — perhaps during the lesson or at some other point during the day. Have them record it in a "Risky Business" journal. Seeing it enumerated and realizing that failure hasn't brought terrible fallout encourages risk-taking on a regular basis. The journal can include sentence starters such as these:

Today I took a risk while _____, I felt _____, and I learned that _____.

Before I take risks I feel _____, and I learned that _____.
During risk-taking, I feel _____, and I learned that _____.
After I've taken a risk I feel _____, and I learned that _____.

Genius Hour and Interest Projects

To promote growth, encourage students to interweave areas they are working on improving with their own interest-based learning. This is a great opportunity for students to work on set goals and provides an opportunity for teachers to address any gaps in their learning by helping to coach them through the process. This will also promote self-worth, risk-taking, and assertiveness, as well as encouraging further goal setting to overcome their barriers. The feeling students get when they have defeated an obstacle is massively liberating and uplifting!

Scope and Scale It

When liberating students to understand that making mistakes and facing adversity is a natural part of learning, we also need to coach them to identify the parameters of their comfort zone and their willingness to fail. Just as investment bankers advise when talking about stock markets and mutual funds, the willingness to take risks is about investing in a plan that can really pay off. Setting these parameters is important to long-term success. Have students identify what risks they are willing to take and record them as goals. Include how you and the student can work together to accomplish these goals. Have them define the risks that — for the moment at least — they are *not* willing to take. Often if a student doesn't finish, or perhaps avoids a task, we tend to blame them without thinking about their readiness to take risks. Avoid the blame game by openly communicating about realistic plans to achieve goals.

I had a student who refused to speak in front of a group of people; she was only comfortable speaking directly with me. Her fear of saying the wrong thing and being made fun of was limiting her. As her coach/guide/educator, I had her define who she would be willing to start sharing ideas with if she was ever going to get past this fear of failing. She was able to identify one student, and so we started there. I also had her define what she was absolutely *not comfortable* with, and she said it would be impossible for her to ever speak at or host an assembly. As we worked on the goal of sharing with one student, her comfort level grew.

Soon she was willing to share in a group of three. As we communicated about our progress, we realized that we needed to define the speaker and listener roles and responsibilities because she was constantly being cut off. This was an opportunity to have her share this idea with the entire class as a good strategy for everyone. Over time she became more comfortable, and in the end, was able to introduce our class at one of the year-end assemblies — an astronomical hurdle for her to have overcome. All of this was possible because we were able to define the scope and boundaries of her fear of failure.

This hold true with adults and teachers too. I once worked with a teacher who was afraid to speak in front of their peers. The administrator was able to help them define the limitations of their public speaking and slowly was able to help that teacher overcome their fear. Learning to fail is not just for our students. It's for all of us.

Chunk It

Break failures down into small chunks, and then analyze specifically what, where, when, and why it happened. Was it the planning, the process, the product, or all of the above that went wrong? Teachers, students, and parents then have a more identifiable entry point to work with that student — purposefully and intentionally — at the appropriate level of learning. Have students pick one thing at which they feel they have recently failed. Then have them do one thing to improve it. In her book, *The Gift of Failure*, Jessica Lahey encourages teachers to focus more on process than product. She confesses this is a tricky balance, especially since schools today are inherently — almost obsessively — focused on product and may inadvertently be contributing to parental anxieties about academic success.

Flop Fridays

This is a fun and easy way to model to students that you too make mistakes. Start Flop Fridays as a way to record what failures and mistakes *you* made during the week that prompted you to learn something new. Openly speak about how it made you feel to fail and how you feel now that you have learned something new because of it. Be sure to include the learning aspect of the process. This is the critical step. It's one thing to talk about, laugh about, and identify failure, but it's useless if we aren't learning from our mistakes.

During a Grade 7 cross-curricular unit at a school I worked at — including science, math, language, French, art, and media literacy — teachers worked together to challenge our students to design, build, market, package, and sell a solar-powered cooker (think small barbeque). This was the first time that seven teachers (myself included as the VP) sat down and planned an integrated unit at this level. We included industry by having investors come in to listen to 30-second elevator pitches, and we had community members show up for our barbeque where the working cookers were on display by being used! Community members were then asked to vote for their favourite design and logo. It was an extremely successful unit, and the many failures upon failures along the way were part of its success. Each student's design was unique and accompanied with its own failures, but in the end, there was a great deal of positive student learning. Table 8.1 presents some of the responses of the teachers about failure and adversity. Table 8.2 has some of the student responses.

Table 8.1

What did you enjoy about this project?	What did you struggle with? What failure or adversity did you face?	What did you learn from that?
Students were more engaged in French because it was an authentic task that connected to what they were learning in other classes. They were able to see the importance of bilingual labelling/ marketing. Students were also more responsible with timelines because their French needed to be finished in order to hand in their brochure in both languages.	Partner absences were sometimes an issue, but we were able to work around it. We were not able to get a native French speaker to come in. Next time, I would like to organize this better.	I learned that even though partner absences were a struggle, the peer learning really benefitted students. Seeing the success of the pitches in one language, I would really like to try to get a French speaker in next year and have them compete for the French market in a similar way.
I really enjoyed the opportunity to collaborate with the other teachers and learn from their experience. I also enjoyed the involvement from the admin.	Partner dynamics changed over the course of the project.	Designate more specific roles. Make a plan with students as to how they will negotiate roles, figure out conflicts, etc.
I really enjoyed how enthusiastic the teachers and students were throughout the entire project. There was a buzz of learning in the school that became contagious and other teams wanted to start to do similar units.	I struggled with keeping the project moving forward given there were outside distractions imposing on the time I wanted and needed for the project. I also struggled with trusting that everyone was sticking to the plan.	I learned that the power of seven minds thinking together for student achievement is very powerful. I learned that it was fun, and that I got to know my colleagues better.

Table 8.2

What was your epic fail?	What did you learn from it?
I think that our epic fail was not really advertising our cooker during the presentation. We kind of just waited there and asked for tickets instead of doing our elevator pitch and advertising our product.	Just something we can work on in the future. We will be more assertive.
Not having a backup plan if the project went sideways, or took too long.	Always have a backup plan!
Getting it to stay together and to look good.	Take more time on the design process.

Failure Fairs

In their book, *Fail Better: Design Smart Mistakes and Succeed Sooner*, Anjali Sastry and Kara Penn pose the question, "Do we celebrate failures or have Failure Fairs? ... We should." This is an interesting concept. Imagine if a school started a Failure Fair; unlike a science fair where things "have to" work, we would encourage students to demonstrate their ideas even if they failed. After all, even the most successful inventors failed far more often than they succeeded. Thomas Edison is thought to have failed between 1,000 and 5,000 times before he invented a commercially viable lightbulb. The business industry thrives on failure and, as John C. Maxwell writes in his book *Failing Forward*, one should fail early, fail often, but always fail forward (Maxwell, 2000). Take FailCon for instance — a conference for start-up founders to learn from and prepare for failure, so they can iterate and grow fast — where stories of entrepreneurial failure are badges of honour (Marcus & Oransky, 2016). Where would we be without the "fail fast, fail often" philosophy? How can you apply this concept in your classroom and at your school?

In the shift towards failure without fear, we are not lowering expectations. In fact, we may even be increasing student, teacher, administrator, and system expectations. The beauty of concluding the book with a series of applicable strategies for daily practice is that you now get to decide what your entry point is in making this shift happen. My own perceptions of what it meant to fail have altered radically. I now know that we grow from those experiences. In my case, they created learning opportunities that made me a better person. I am no longer hesitant to ask questions. I no longer worry about what others may think of me. I am comfortable voicing my opinion to advance an idea, knowing that it may be wrong or not the popular choice. I now embrace challenges as amazing opportunities to learn and add extra tools to my toolkit. I know *my* next steps are to continue to pivot away from fearing failure. What are *your* next steps towards promoting failure without fear?

Ideas to try with colleagues or in the classroom

Define your scope and scale for failure as a launch pad for risk-taking. Record these, and pick a natural next step or risk you are willing to take. Check back biweekly to monitor your progress, and then update your scope and scale accordingly.

Reflect on your learning from reading this book, and decide what strategies are the most impactful for you to implement. Which ones are manageable and achievable within this school year?

Roll up your sleeves, take a deep breath, and allow yourself to jump with both feet towards a Failure Without Fear mindset!

Bibliography

Adams, S. (2013). The 10 skills employers most want in 20-something employees. *Forbes Magazine*, 11 October 2013. Retrieved from https://www.forbes.com/sites/susanadams/2013/10/11/the-10-skills-employers-most-want-in-20-something-employees/#447987886330

Adelman, C. (2005). *Moving into town—and moving on: The community college in the lives of traditional-age students.* Washington, DC: U.S. Department of Education. Retrieved from https://www2.ed.gov/rschstat/research/pubs/comcollege/movingintotown.pdf

Bachman, J. G., O'Malley, P. M., Schulenberg, J. E., Johnston, L. D., Fredoman-Doan, P., & Messersmith, E. E. (2008). *The education-drug use connection: How successes and failures in school relate to adolescent smoking, drinking, drug use and delinquency.* New York: Taylor & Francis

Baum, N. L. (2005). Building resilience: A school-based intervention for children exposed to ongoing trauma and stress. *Journal of Aggression, Maltreatment & Trauma, 10*(1–2), 487–498. DOI:10.1300/J146v10n01_08

Bayless, K. (n.d.). What is helicopter parenting? *Parenting Magazine.* Retrieved from https://www.parents.com/parenting/better-parenting/what-is-helicopter-parenting/

Bennett, B., & Rolheiser, C. (2002). *Beyond Monet: The artful science of instructional integration.* Toronto: Bookation.

Berger, W. (n.d.). Why do kids ask so many questions—and why do they stop? A More Beautiful Question. Retrieved from https://amorebeautifulquestion.com/why-do-kids-ask-so-many-questions-but-more-importantly-why-do-they-stop/

Bernard, N. S., Dollinger, S. J., & Ramaniah, N. V. (2002). Applying the big five personality factors to the impostor phenomenon. *Journal of Personality Assessment, 78*, 321–333. DOI:10.1207/S15327752JPA7802_07

Bowermaster, D. (2016). New evidence of growth mindset's positive effect on achievement on a national scale—especially for low-income students. Mindset Scholars Network, 22 July 2016. Retrieved from http://mindsetscholarsnetwork.org/new-evidence-growth-mindsets-positive-effect-achievement-national-scale-especially-low-income-students/

Buck Institute for Education. (2019). What is PBL? PBL Works. Retrieved from https://www.pblworks.org/what-is-pbl

Canadian Parents for French (Ontario). (2019). The State of French Second Language (FSL) Education in Ontario. Retrieved from https://on.cpf.ca/wp-content/blogs.dir/1/files/State-of-FSL-Education-in-Ontario-February-2019.pdf

Chernyak, P. (n.d.). How to develop a flexible mindset. Wikihow. Retrieved from https://www.wikihow.com/Develop-a-Flexible-Mindset

Clance, P. R. (1985). *The impostor phenomenon: Overcoming the fear that haunts your success.* Atlanta, GA: Peachtree Publishers.

Clance, P. R., & Imes, S. A. (1978). The impostor phenomenon in high achieving women: Dynamics and therapeutic intervention. *Psychotherapy: Theory, Research, and Practice, 15*(3), 241–247.

Coelho, E. (2004). *Adding English.* Don Mills, ON: Pippin Publishing.

Conroy, D. E., Kaye, M. P., Fifer, A. M. (2007). Cognitive links between fear of failure and perfectionism. *Journal of Rational-Emotive & Cognitive-Behavior Therapy, 25*(4), 237–253.

De Castella, K., Byrne, D., & Covington, M. (2013). Unmotivated or motivated to fail? A cross-cultural study of achievement motivation, fear of failure, and student disengagement. *Journal of Educational Psychology, 105*(3), 861–880.

Dickinson, K. (2018). Video games and the paradox of failure. *Big Think*, 10 December 2018. Retrieved from https://bigthink.com/personal-growth/play-video-games-to-fail

Donohoo, J. (2013). *Collaborative inquiry for educators: A facilitator's guide to school improvement.* Thousand Oaks, CA: Corwin.

Donatone, K. (2013). Why millennials can't grow up: Helicopter parenting has caused my psychotherapy clients to crash land. *Slate*, 2 December 2013. Retrieved from https://slate.com/technology/2013/12/millennial-narcissism-helicopter-parents-are-college-students-bigger-problem.html

Dowshen, S. (February, 2015). Childhood Stress. Kids Health, the Nemours Foundation. Retrieved from https://kidshealth.org/en/parents/stress.html

Duckworth, A. (2013, April). Grit: The power of passion and perseverance. Ted Talks Education. Retrieved from https://www.ted.com/talks/angela_lee_duckworth_grit_the_power_of_passion_and_perseverance

Dweck, C. (2006). *Mindset: The new psychology of success.* New York: Random House.

Dweck, C. (2010). Even geniuses work hard. *Educational Leadership, 68*(1), 16–20.

Dweck, C. (2012). Mindset—What is it? Retrieved from https://mindsetonline.com/whatisit/about/index.html

Dweck, C. (2016). Recognizing and overcoming false growth mindset. *Edutopia,* 11 January 2016. Retrieved from https://www.edutopia.org/blog/recognizing-overcoming-false-growth-mindset-carol-dweck

Dweck, C. S., Walton, G. M., & Cohen, G. L. (2014). Academic tenacity: Mindsets and skills that promote long-term learning. Bill & Melinda Gates Foundation. https://ed.stanford.edu/sites/default/files/manual/dweck-walton-cohen-2014.pdf

EurekAlert. (2018, July 9). Motivating gamers with personalized game design. University of Waterloo. Retrieved from www.eurkalert.org/pub_releases/2018-07/uow070618.php

Fagell, P. (2016). 10 ways to help kids take risks in a world of 'no's'. *Washington Post,* 21 June 2016. Retrieved from https://www.washingtonpost.com/news/parenting/wp/2016/06/21/10-ways-to-help-kids-take-risks-in-a-world-of-nos/?utm_term=.ce5024e782d9

Farber, M. (2016). 3 ways to use game-based learning. Edutopia. Retrieved from https://www.edutopia.org/article/3-ways-use-game-based-learning-matthew-farber

Freudenberg, N., & Ruglis, J. (2007). Reframing school dropout as a public health issue. *Preventing Chronic Disease: Public Health Research, Practice, and Policy, 4,* 1–11.

Genesee, F., Lindholm-Leary, K., Saunders, W., & Christian, D. (2006). *Educating English language learners: A synthesis of research evidence.* New York: Cambridge University Press.

Gini-Newman, G. (2014). Cascading curriculum: A choreographed approach to student inquiry. Retrieved from https://www.nesacenter.org/uploaded/conferences/WTI/2014/handouts/Garfield_Gini-Newman/B-Cascading_Handbook.pdf

Ginott, H. G. (1971). *Between parent and teenager.* New York: Avon.

Goleman, D. (2005). *Emotional intelligence: 10th anniversary edition; Why it can matter more than IQ.* New York: Bantam Books.

Grant, G. M. (2012). Why kids need to fail to succeed in school. *Globe and Mail*, 31 August 2012. https://www.theglobeandmail.com/life/parenting/back-to-school/why-kids-need-to-fail-to-succeed-in-school/article4513436/

Gross, K. (2017). Let's think differently about change to understand why it's so difficult. The Aspen Institute, 12 July 2017. Retrieved from https://www.aspeninstitute.org/blog-posts/lets-think-differently-about-change-to-understand-why-its-so-difficult/

Harris, P. (2015). How many jobs should you expect to hold in your lifetime? Workopolis. Retrieved from https://careers.workopolis.com/advice/how-many-jobs-should-you-expect-to-hold-in-your-lifetime/

Hamre, B. K., & Pianta, R. C. (2005). Can instructional and emotional support in the first-grade classroom make a difference for children at risk of school failure? *Child Development, 76*(5), 949–967.

Hamre, B. K., Pianta, R. C., Downer, J. T., & Mashburn, A. J. (2005). Teachers' perceptions of conflict with young students: Looking beyond problem behaviors. *Social Development, 17*(1), 115–136.

Hanley-Dafoe, R. (2019). How to foster resiliency within ourselves. Speakers' Spotlight blog post. Retrieved from https://www.speakers.ca/2019/09/dr-robyne-hanley-dafoe-how-to-foster-resiliency-within-ourselves/

Hannay, L., Wideman, R., & Seller, W. (2010). Professional learning to reshape teaching. Toronto, ON: Elementary Teachers' Federation of Ontario.

Hastings, S. (2003). Questioning. Retrieved from http://teachertools.londongt.org/en-GB/resources/Questions_article_tes.doc

Hazell, W. (2017). Hattie on Dweck: Sometimes pupils need "fixed mindsets," argues leading academic. TES, 29 June 2017. Retrieved from https://www.tes.com/news/school-news/breaking-news/hattie-dweck-sometimes-pupils-need-fixed-mindsets-argues-leading

Hewitt, P. L., & Flett, G. L. (1991). Perfectionism in the self and social contexts: Conceptualization, assessment, and association with psychopathology. *Journal of Personality and Social Psychology, 60*(3), 456–470. DOI:10.1037/0022-3514.60.3.456

Hewitt, P. L., Flett, G. L., & Turnbull-Donovan, W. (1992). Perfectionism and suicide potential. *British Journal of Clinical Psychology, 31,* 181–190.

ISTE (International Society for Technology in Education). (2019a). ISTE Standards. Retrieved from https://www.iste.org/standards

ISTE (International Society for Technology in Education). (2019b). ISTE Standards for Educators. Retrieved from https://www.iste.org/standards/for-educators

ISTE (International Society for Technology in Education). (2019c). ISTE Standards for Students. Retrieved from https://www.iste.org/standards/for-students

Jennings, P. (2015). Seven ways mindfulness can help teachers. *Greater Good Magazine*, 30 March 2015. Retrieved from https://greatergood.berkeley.edu/article/item/seven_ways_mindfulness_can help teachers

Jobs, S. (1995, April 20). Smithsonian Institution oral history interview. Retrieved from http://americanhistory.si.edu/comphist/sj1.html

Keating, D. (2017). Dealing with stress at school in an age of anxiety: Building a culture of resilience at school counters a growing stress epidemic. *Psychology Today*, 15 August 2017. Retrieved from https://www.psychologytoday.com/us/blog/stressful-lives/201708/dealing-stress-school-in-age-anxiety

Keller, A. (2013). What we did when our son was failing school. Penelope Trunk, 30 April 2013. Retrieved from http://education.penelopetrunk.com/2013/04/30/what-we-did-when-our-son-was-failing-school/

Killoran, I., & Bliss, S. R. (2107). Mindfulness in education: Using and teaching mindfulness in schools. *Childhood Education, 93*(2), 99.

Kindlon, D., & Thompson, M. (1999). Raising Cain: Protecting the Emotional Life of Boys. New York: Ballantine Books.

Kolb, L. (2015). Epic fail or win? Gamifying learning in my classroom. *Edutopia*, 20 March 2015. Retrieved from https://www.edutopia.org/blog/epic-fail-win-gamifying-learning-liz-kolb

Kumar, M. (2014). A simple guide to teaching resilience. Hub Pages, 27 October 2016. Retrieved from https://hubpages.com/education/A-Simple-Guide-to-Teaching-Resilience

Lechner, T. (2018). Resilience and grit: How to develop a growth mindset. The Chopra Center. Retrieved from http://www.chopra.com/articles/resilience-and-grit-how-to-develop-a-growth-mindset#sm.00000ueaxgehasfjlr9e8xhp26f4r

Lovell, K. (2017). Coding is the new cursive writing — and we have to embrace it. *Globe and Mail*, 23 July 2017. Retrieved from https://www.theglobeandmail.com/opinion/coding-is-the-new-cursive-writing-and-we-have-to-embrace-it/article35776671/

Marcus, A., & Oransky, I. (2016). Why scientists should learn to fail, fast and often. Stat News, 12 May 2016. Retrieved from https://www.statnews.com/2016/05/12/failure-scientists/

Matthews, G., & Clance, P. (1985). Treatment of the impostor phenomenon in psychotherapy clients. *Psychotherapy in Private Practice, 3*(1), 71–81.

Maxwell, J. C. (2000). *Failing forward: Turning mistakes into stepping stones for success.* Nashville, TN: Thomas Nelson Publishers.

Maynard, B. R., Sala-Wright, C. P., & Vaughn, M. G. (2015). High school dropouts in emerging adulthood: Substance use, mental health problems, and crime. *Community Mental Health, 51,* 289–299. DOI:10.1007/s10597-014-9760-5

McClelland, D. (n.d.). Need theory. Revolvy. Retrieved from https://www.revolvy.com/page/Need-theory

McGonigal, J. (2011). *Reality is broken: Why games make us better and how they can change the world.* New York: Penguin Group.

Michou, A., Vansteenkiste, M., Mouratidis, A., & Lens, W. (2014). Enriching the hierarchical model of achievement motivation: Autonomous and controlling reasons underlying achievement goals. *British Journal of Educational Psychology, 84*(4), 650–666. DOI:10.1111/bjep.12055

Miller, A. (2013). Canadian students feel stress, anxiety, have suicidal thoughts, survey reveals. *Globe and Mail,* 17 June 2013. Retrieved from https://www.theglobeandmail.com/news/national/education/college-university-students-feel-stress-anxiety-have-suicidal-thoughts-survey-reveals/article12613742/

Moser, J. S., Schroder, H. S., Heeter, C., Moran, T. P., & Lee, Y. H. (2011). Mind your errors: Evidence for a neural mechanism linking growth mind-set to adaptive post-error adjustments. *Psychological Science, 22*(12), 1484–1489. DOI:0956797611419520

Munsey, C. (2010). The kids aren't all right: New data from APA's Stress in America survey indicate parents don't know what's bothering their children. *Monitor on Psychology 41*(1), 22. Retrieved from http://www.apa.org/monitor/2010/01/stress-kids.aspx

Nair, R. (2017, January 30). Sea to Sky school district to pilot grade-less report cards: Pilot program — which will launch in spring — will change report cards for some students in Grades 4 to 9. CBC News. Retrieved from https://www.cbc.ca/news/canada/british-co-lumbia/sea-to-sky-school-district-to-pilot-grade-less-report-cards-1.3957985

Northeast Foundation for Children. (2019). Principles and practices. Responsive Classroom. Retrieved from https://www.responsiveclassroom.org/about/principles-practices/

Ontario Ministry of Education (2005). *Many roots, many voices: Supporting English language learners in every classroom. A practical guide for Ontario educators.* Toronto.

Ontario Ministry of Education. (2008). *Supporting English language learners: A practical guide for supporting English language learners grades 1–8.* Toronto.

Ontario Ministry of Education. (2010a). *Growing success: Assessment, evaluation and reporting in Ontario's schools: Covering grades 1 to 12.* Toronto.

Ontario Ministry of Education. (2010b). *New teacher induction program.* Toronto: Queen's Printer for Ontario.

Ontario Ministry of Education. (2011, July). Asking effective questions. Capacity Building Series, special edition #21. Toronto, ON. Retrieved from http://www.edu.gov.on.ca/eng/literacynumeracy/inspire/research/cbs_askingeffectivequestions.pdf

Palumbo, R. V., Marraccini, M. E., Weyandt, L. L., Wilder-Smith, O., McGee, H. A., Liu, S., & Goodwin, M. S. (2017). Interpersonal autonomic physiology: A systematic review of the literature. *Personality and Social Psychology Review, 21*(2), 99–141.

Pianta, R. C., Hamre, B. K., & Allen, J. P. (2012). Teacher–student relationships and engagement: Conceptualizing, measuring, and improving the capacity of classroom interactions. In S. L. Christenson, A. L. Reschly, & C. Wylie (Eds.), *Handbook of research on student engagement* (pp. 365–386). New York: Springer Science + Business Media. DOI:10.1007/978-1-4614-2018-7_17

Przeworski, A. (2013). 12 tips to reduce your child's stress and anxiety: Parenting an anxious or stressed child. *Psychology Today,* 19 February 2013. https://www.psychologytoday.com/us/blog/dont-worry-mom/201302/12-tips-reduce-your-childs-stress-and-anxiety

Reynolds, J., Stewart, M., Macdonald, R., & Sischo, L. (2006). Have adolescents become too ambitious? High school seniors' educational and occupational plans, 1976 to 2000. *Social Problems*, 53, 186–206. DOI:10.1525/sp.2006.53.2.186

Romano, R. M., & Palmer, J. C. (2015). *Financing community colleges: Where we are, where we're going* (The Futures Series on Community Colleges). Lanham, MD: Rowman & Littlefield Publishers.

Romero, C. (2015, July). What we know about growth mindset from scientific research. Mindset Scholars Network. http://mindsetscholarsnetwork.org/wp-content/uploads/2015/09/What-We-Know-About-Growth-Mindset.pdf

Rowe, J. (2014). How kids experience stress. Australian Government Department of Health. Retrieved from https://beyou.edu.au/fact-sheets/your-wellbeing/stress-management

Rowling, J. K. (2017). Text of J. K. Rowling's speech. *Harvard Gazette*. Retrieved from http://news.harvard.edu/gazette/story/2008/06/text-of-j-k-rowling-speech/?utm_source=twitter&utm_medium=social&utm_campaign=hu-twitter-general

Sakulku, J., & Alexander, J. (2011). The impostor phenomenon. *International Journal of Behavioral Science, 6*(1), 73–92.

Sastry, A., & Penn, K. (2014). *Fail better: Design smart mistakes and succeed sooner*. Brighton, MA: Harvard Business Review Press.

Scott, S. (2007). Do grades really matter? A growing body of evidence suggests grades don't predict success: C+ students are the ones who end up running the world. *Maclean's Magazine*, 30 August 2007. https://www.macleans.ca/education/uniandcollege/do-grades-really-matter/

Senge, P. M. (2006). *The fifth discipline: The art and practice of the learning organization* (revised edition). New York/Toronto: Doubleday Publishing.

Swain, R. C., Beauvais, F., Chavez, E. L., & Oetting, E. R. (1997). The effect of dropout rates on estimates of adolescent substance use among three racial/ethnic groups. *American Journal of Public Health, 87,* 51–55. DOI:10.2105/AJPH.87.1.51

Thompson, M. (2000). *Speaking of boys: Answers to the most-asked questions about raising sons.* New York: Ballantine Books.

Townsend, L., Flisher, A. J., & King, G. (2007). A systematic review of the relationship between high school dropout and substance use. *Clinical Child and Family Psychology, 10,* 295–317. DOI:10.1007/s10567-007-0023-7

VanLeeuwen, D. (2017). Seven steps to becoming a moon-shooter and blasting your way to the top. Retrieved from https://www.deanvanleeuwen-members.com/seven-steps-becoming-moonshooter-blasting-value-sky-high/

Wichstrøm, L. (1998). Alcohol intoxication and school dropout. *Drug and Alcohol Review, 17,* 413–421. DOI:10.1080/09595239800187251

Wiggins, G. (2012). Seven keys to effective feedback. *Educational Leadership, 70*(1), 10–16. Retrieved from http://www.ascd.org/publications/educational-leadership/sept12/vol70/num01/Seven-Keys-to-Effective-Feedback.aspx

About the Author

Chad has been an elementary Curriculum Leader supporting educators as an instructional coach in the areas of Equity and Inclusion, FNMI, Student Success, Science and Technology, and English as a Second Language. He also had the opportunity to work with the Perimeter Institute in Waterloo, Ontario, to write and design cross-curricular math and science units for grades 5 to 8.

Working with the Ministry of Education as a Student Work–Study Teacher, Chad has done grass-roots research in numeracy and literacy by working alongside students to help them identify gaps and suggesting strategies to close those gaps. From all these experiences, he has developed his philosophy that failure is just another form of fertilizer that helps us grow and learn.

Made in the USA
Lexington, KY
17 December 2019